From Chaos To Control: How To Develop Strong Executive functioning Skills

Travis Breeding

Published by Travis Breeding, 2024.

While every precaution has been taken in the preparation of this book, the publisher assumes no responsibility for errors or omissions, or for damages resulting from the use of the information contained herein.

FROM CHAOS TO CONTROL: HOW TO DEVELOP STRONG EXECUTIVE FUNCTIONING SKILLS

First edition. February 20, 2024.

Copyright © 2024 Travis Breeding.

ISBN: 979-8224542949

Written by Travis Breeding.

Also by Travis Breeding

Harmony in Flux: Navigating Bi-Polar Brilliance

The Friendship Rainbow

The Great Kindergarten Adventure: A Story about Going to School with Autism

The Magic Forest Adventure

Unlocking Brilliance: Navigating Autism and Applied Behavior Analysis Towards a Radiant Future

Decoding Love: Navigating Dating and Relationships on the Autism Spectrum

Echoes of a Late Diagnosis: Unveiling the Spectrum Within

From Theory to Practice: Implementing Effective Autism Interventions St

The Amazing Adventures of Aiden and His Asperger's Superpowers

The Magical Adventures of Lily and the Enchanted Forest

Unlocking Potential: A Journey Of Discovery Through ABA Therapy

Unlocking Potential: Navigating Employment for Neurodiverse Talent

Unlocking the Spectrum: A Journey through Applied Behavior Analysis from an Autistic Perspective

Unlocking The Spectrum: Navigating The Complexity Of Autism With Advanced Strategies And Insights

Beyond The Spectrum: Insights From Autistic Adults

Beyond The Stereotypes

Breaking Barriers: Navigating Autism With Therapeutic Insight

Celebrating Neurodiversity

Watch for more at breedingautismconsulting.com.

Table of Contents

Chapter 1: How to Build Strong Relationships with Your Coworkers

Building strong relationships with coworkers is essential for a successful and fulfilling career. When we have positive relationships with our colleagues, it not only increases job satisfaction but also improves productivity and creates a more positive work environment. In this article, we will explore the importance of building strong relationships with coworkers and provide tips on how to develop effective communication skills, build trust and respect, create a positive work environment, find common ground, balance personal and professional relationships, resolve conflicts, show appreciation and recognition, network and collaborate, maintain boundaries and professionalism, and sustain strong relationships over time.

Understanding the Importance of Building Strong Relationships with Coworkers

Having strong relationships with coworkers has numerous benefits. Firstly, it increases job satisfaction. When we have positive interactions with our colleagues, we are more likely to enjoy our work and feel fulfilled in our roles. Additionally, strong relationships with coworkers can lead to increased productivity. When we have good relationships with those we work with, we are more likely to collaborate effectively, share ideas, and support each other in achieving common goals.

Furthermore, building strong relationships with coworkers creates a more positive work environment. When there is trust and respect among colleagues, it fosters a sense of camaraderie and teamwork. This positive atmosphere can lead to higher morale, reduced stress levels, and improved overall well-being in the workplace.

Developing Communication Skills to Connect with Coworkers

Effective communication is crucial in building relationships with coworkers. It allows us to understand each other better, resolve conflicts, and collaborate effectively. To improve communication skills, it is important to practice active listening. This means giving our full attention to the person speaking, maintaining eye contact, and asking clarifying questions to ensure understanding.

Clear communication is also essential in building strong relationships. It is important to express ourselves clearly and concisely, using appropriate language and tone. Being mindful of non-verbal cues such as body language and facial expressions can also enhance communication and help us connect with our coworkers on a deeper level.

Building Trust and Respect with Coworkers

Trust and respect are the foundation of strong relationships with coworkers. Without these elements, it is difficult to build meaningful connections. To build trust, it is important to be reliable and follow through on commitments. This means delivering work on time, being accountable for our actions, and being consistent in our behavior.

Respect is equally important in building strong relationships. It involves treating others with kindness, empathy, and consideration.

Respecting boundaries, listening to others' opinions, and valuing diversity are all ways to demonstrate respect in the workplace.

Creating a Positive Work Environment to Foster Strong Relationships

A positive work environment is essential for building strong relationships with coworkers. It creates a sense of belonging, encourages collaboration, and boosts morale. To create a positive work environment, it is important to show appreciation and recognition for coworkers' contributions. This can be done through simple gestures such as saying thank you, giving compliments, or publicly acknowledging achievements.

Additionally, fostering open communication and encouraging teamwork can contribute to a positive work environment. Creating opportunities for social interaction, such as team-building activities or lunchtime gatherings, can also help build camaraderie among coworkers.

Finding Common Ground with Coworkers

Finding common ground with coworkers is crucial in building strong relationships. It allows us to connect on a personal level and find shared interests or goals. To find common ground, it is important to take the time to get to know our colleagues beyond their professional roles.

Engaging in conversations about hobbies, interests, or current events can help us discover shared passions or experiences. Additionally, finding common goals or projects to collaborate on can strengthen relationships and create a sense of unity among coworkers.

Balancing Personal and Professional Relationships with Coworkers

Balancing personal and professional relationships with coworkers can be challenging. While it is important to build strong relationships, it is equally important to maintain professionalism and boundaries in the workplace. To achieve this balance, it is important to be mindful of the context and setting.

Maintaining professionalism means avoiding gossip, refraining from discussing personal matters in a professional setting, and respecting personal space. It is also important to be aware of power dynamics and avoid favoritism or conflicts of interest that may arise from personal relationships.

Resolving Conflicts and Disagreements with Coworkers

Conflicts and disagreements are inevitable in any workplace. However, it is important to address and resolve them in a constructive manner to maintain strong relationships with coworkers. Active listening is key in resolving conflicts. It involves giving our full attention to the other person's perspective, seeking to understand their point of view, and finding common ground.

Finding common ground can help bridge differences and find mutually beneficial solutions. It is also important to approach conflicts with empathy and respect, focusing on the issue at hand rather than personal attacks. Seeking mediation or involving a neutral third party can also be helpful in resolving conflicts.

Showing Appreciation and Recognition for Coworkers

Showing appreciation and recognition for coworkers is essential in building strong relationships. It not only boosts morale but also strengthens the sense of camaraderie and teamwork. Simple gestures such as saying thank you, giving compliments, or expressing gratitude can go a long way in showing appreciation.

Publicly acknowledging coworkers' achievements or contributions can also be impactful. This can be done through team meetings, company-wide emails, or social media platforms. Additionally, providing opportunities for professional growth and development can show that we value our coworkers' skills and contributions.

Networking and Collaborating with Coworkers

Networking and collaborating with coworkers can have numerous benefits for our careers. It allows us to expand our professional network, learn from others' expertise, and discover new opportunities. To network and collaborate effectively, it is important to attend company events, industry conferences, or professional development workshops.

Volunteering for projects or cross-functional teams can also provide opportunities for collaboration and networking. Additionally, being open to sharing knowledge and skills with coworkers can foster a culture of collaboration and support in the workplace.

Maintaining Boundaries and Professionalism with Coworkers

Maintaining boundaries and professionalism with coworkers is crucial in building strong relationships. It ensures that personal relationships do not interfere with professional responsibilities and that everyone feels respected and valued in the workplace. To maintain boundaries, it is important to avoid gossip or discussing personal matters in a professional setting.

Respecting personal space and privacy is also essential. It is important to be mindful of others' boundaries and not overstep them. Additionally, being aware of power dynamics and avoiding conflicts of interest can help maintain professionalism in relationships with coworkers.

Sustaining Strong Relationships with Coworkers Over Time

Building strong relationships with coworkers is an ongoing process that requires effort and commitment. To sustain relationships over time, it is important to stay in touch with coworkers even outside of work-related interactions. This can be done through social events, coffee breaks, or virtual hangouts.

Continuing to show appreciation and recognition for coworkers' contributions is also important in sustaining relationships. Additionally, being supportive and offering help when needed can strengthen relationships and foster a sense of trust and camaraderie.

Building strong relationships with coworkers is essential for a successful and fulfilling career. It increases job satisfaction, improves productivity, and creates a positive work environment. By developing effective communication skills, building trust and respect, creating a positive work environment, finding common ground, balancing personal and professional relationships, resolving conflicts, showing appreciation and recognition, networking and collaborating, maintaining boundaries and professionalism, and sustaining relationships over time, we can build stronger relationships with our coworkers. Implementing these tips will not only enhance our professional lives but also contribute to a more positive and fulfilling work experience.

Chapter 2: From Struggle to Success: The Role of Support in Overcoming Challenges

Life is full of challenges, and at times, it can feel overwhelming to face them alone. That's where support comes in. Having a strong support system can make all the difference in overcoming obstacles and achieving success. Support can come in many forms, from emotional and practical assistance to financial and professional guidance. In this article, we will explore the different types of support and how they can help individuals overcome challenges.

Understanding the Different Types of Support

Support can be categorized into various types, each playing a crucial role in helping individuals overcome challenges. Emotional support involves providing comfort, empathy, and understanding to someone going through a difficult time. Practical support refers to tangible assistance, such as helping with daily tasks or providing resources to solve problems. Financial support involves providing monetary assistance to alleviate financial burdens. Professional support entails seeking guidance from experts or mentors in a specific field. Social support involves connecting with others who share similar experiences or interests. Lastly, self-support refers to the ability to rely on oneself for motivation and resilience.

The Role of Emotional Support in Overcoming Challenges

Emotional support is vital in helping individuals overcome challenges because it provides a sense of comfort and validation. When facing difficulties, having someone who listens without judgment and offers empathy can make a significant difference in one's ability to cope. Emotional support can come from friends, family members, or even support groups where individuals can share their experiences and find solace in knowing they are not alone.

For example, someone going through a divorce may find emotional support from a close friend who listens to their concerns and offers words of encouragement. This emotional support can help them navigate the emotional rollercoaster that comes with the end of a marriage.

The Benefits of Practical Support in Overcoming Challenges

Practical support is equally important in overcoming challenges because it provides tangible assistance that helps individuals address their problems more effectively. This type of support can come in the form of someone helping with household chores, running errands, or providing transportation. Practical support can also involve offering resources or advice to help individuals find solutions to their problems.

For instance, a single parent who is struggling to balance work and childcare responsibilities may benefit from practical support in the form of a neighbor or family member who offers to babysit or help with household chores. This practical assistance can alleviate some of the stress and allow the parent to focus on their work and other responsibilities.

The Importance of Financial Support in Overcoming Challenges

Financial support plays a significant role in overcoming challenges, especially when individuals are facing financial hardships. It can provide the means to access necessary resources, such as healthcare, education, or housing. Financial support can come from various sources, including family members, friends, charitable organizations, or government assistance programs.

For example, a student from a low-income background may receive financial support in the form of scholarships or grants that enable them to pursue higher education. This financial assistance can open doors to opportunities that would otherwise be out of reach.

The Role of Professional Support in Overcoming Challenges

Professional support is crucial in overcoming challenges because it provides individuals with expert guidance and advice. Professionals in various fields, such as therapists, coaches, mentors, or career counselors, can offer valuable insights and strategies to help individuals navigate their challenges more effectively.

For instance, someone struggling with anxiety may seek professional support from a therapist who can provide them with coping mechanisms and tools to manage their symptoms. This professional guidance can empower individuals to overcome their challenges and improve their overall well-being.

The Impact of Social Support in Overcoming Challenges

Social support is essential in overcoming challenges because it provides individuals with a sense of belonging and community. Connecting with others who have similar experiences or interests can offer a valuable support network where individuals can share advice, encouragement, and resources.

For example, someone dealing with the loss of a loved one may find solace in a grief support group where they can connect with others who have gone through similar experiences. This social support can provide a safe space for individuals to express their emotions and receive understanding from others who can relate.

The Power of Self-Support in Overcoming Challenges

While external support is crucial, self-support is equally important in overcoming challenges. Self-support involves developing resilience, self-motivation, and self-care practices that help individuals navigate difficult times. It is about recognizing one's own strengths and abilities and using them to overcome obstacles.

For instance, someone facing a career setback may practice self-support by setting goals, staying positive, and seeking opportunities for growth and learning. By relying on their own inner strength and determination, they can overcome the challenges they face and come out stronger on the other side.

Strategies for Building a Support System

Building a support system is essential for overcoming challenges. Here are some strategies to help individuals build a strong support network:

1. Identify your needs: Reflect on the types of support you need and the areas where you could benefit from assistance.

2. Reach out to friends and family: Share your challenges with trusted friends and family members who can offer emotional support and practical assistance.

3. Join support groups: Seek out support groups or communities where you can connect with others who share similar experiences or interests.

4. Seek professional guidance: Consider reaching out to professionals in relevant fields who can provide expert advice and guidance.

5. Give back: Be willing to offer support to others in need, as this can create reciprocal relationships and strengthen your own support system.

Overcoming Common Challenges in Seeking Support

While seeking support is crucial, there are common challenges that individuals may face when reaching out for help. These challenges include fear of judgment, feelings of vulnerability, or difficulty asking for assistance. To overcome these challenges, individuals can:

1. Practice self-compassion: Remember that it is okay to ask for help and that everyone faces challenges at some point in their lives.

2. Seek out trusted individuals: Reach out to people you trust and feel comfortable sharing your challenges with.

3. Be specific about your needs: Clearly communicate what type of support you are seeking, whether it is emotional, practical, or financial.

4. Educate yourself: Learn about available resources and support networks in your community or online.

5. Take small steps: Start by seeking support from one person or joining a small support group before expanding your network.

The Transformative Power of Support in Achieving Success

In conclusion, support plays a crucial role in helping individuals overcome challenges and achieve success. Whether it is emotional, practical, financial, professional, social, or self-support, each type of support offers unique benefits that can make a significant difference in one's ability to navigate difficult times. Building a strong support system and reaching out for assistance when needed is essential for personal growth and resilience. So, remember to lean on your support system when facing challenges, as they can provide the encouragement, guidance, and resources necessary to overcome obstacles and achieve success.

Chapter 3: How to Boost Your Job Satisfaction and Achieve Career Fulfillment

Job satisfaction is a crucial aspect of our professional lives. It refers to the level of contentment and fulfillment that individuals experience in their jobs. When employees are satisfied with their work, they are more likely to be engaged, motivated, and productive. Job satisfaction also has a significant impact on overall well-being and mental health. In this article, we will explore the importance of job satisfaction and provide tips on how to enhance it.

Understanding the Importance of Job Satisfaction

Job satisfaction is defined as the positive emotional state resulting from an individual's appraisal of their job or job experiences. It encompasses various factors such as the nature of work, relationships with colleagues and superiors, compensation, and opportunities for growth and development.

When employees are satisfied with their jobs, they are more likely to be committed to their organizations and have higher levels of productivity. They are also more likely to experience lower levels of stress and burnout. Job satisfaction has been linked to increased job performance, reduced turnover rates, and improved overall well-being.

On the other hand, job dissatisfaction can have detrimental effects on both individuals and organizations. Employees who are dissatisfied with their jobs may experience decreased motivation, lower productivity, and higher rates of absenteeism. They may also be more prone to physical and mental health issues such as anxiety and depression.

Identifying Your Career Goals

Setting clear career goals is essential for job satisfaction. When individuals have a sense of direction and purpose in their careers, they are more likely to feel fulfilled and motivated in their work.

To identify your career goals, start by reflecting on your interests, values, and skills. Consider what you enjoy doing and what you are passionate about. Think about your long-term aspirations and where you see yourself in the future. It can also be helpful to seek guidance from mentors or career counselors who can provide insights and support in the goal-setting process.

Assessing Your Current Job Satisfaction Level

Assessing your current job satisfaction level is crucial for understanding what aspects of your job are contributing to your satisfaction or dissatisfaction. By identifying areas of improvement, you can take steps to enhance your job satisfaction.

There are various methods for assessing job satisfaction. One common approach is to use surveys or questionnaires that measure different dimensions of job satisfaction, such as work-life balance, compensation, and opportunities for growth. Another method is to engage in self-reflection and journaling to explore your feelings and thoughts about your job.

Analyzing the Factors Affecting Your Job Satisfaction

Several factors can influence job satisfaction. By analyzing these factors, you can gain insights into what aspects of your job are contributing to your satisfaction or dissatisfaction.

Common factors affecting job satisfaction include the nature of work, relationships with colleagues and superiors, compensation and benefits, work-life balance, and opportunities for growth and development. It is essential to assess each of these factors and determine which ones are most important to you.

To analyze the factors affecting your job satisfaction, consider keeping a journal where you can reflect on your experiences at work. Take note of the tasks that bring you joy and fulfillment, as well as the ones that drain your energy. Pay attention to the relationships you have with your colleagues and superiors and how they impact your overall satisfaction.

Building Positive Relationships with Colleagues and Superiors

Positive relationships at work play a significant role in job satisfaction. When individuals have supportive and collaborative relationships with their colleagues and superiors, they are more likely to feel valued and motivated in their jobs.

To build positive relationships at work, start by being respectful and considerate towards your colleagues and superiors. Show appreciation for their contributions and offer support when needed.

Foster open communication by actively listening to others and expressing your thoughts and ideas clearly.

It is also important to be a team player and collaborate effectively with others. By working together towards common goals, you can create a positive and supportive work environment.

Creating a Healthy Work-Life Balance

Achieving a healthy work-life balance is crucial for job satisfaction. When individuals have time for their personal lives and hobbies, they are more likely to feel fulfilled and satisfied in their jobs.

To create a healthy work-life balance, set boundaries between your work and personal life. Establish specific times for work and leisure activities and stick to them as much as possible. Prioritize self-care by engaging in activities that help you relax and recharge.

It is also important to communicate your needs and expectations with your colleagues and superiors. Let them know when you need time off or when you are feeling overwhelmed. By advocating for yourself, you can create a work environment that supports your well-being.

Seeking Professional Development Opportunities

Professional development is essential for job satisfaction. When individuals have opportunities to learn and grow in their careers, they are more likely to feel engaged and motivated in their work.

To seek professional development opportunities, start by identifying your areas of interest and areas for improvement. Consider attending workshops, conferences, or seminars related to your field. Take advantage of online courses or certifications that can enhance your skills and knowledge.

It is also important to seek feedback from your colleagues and superiors. Ask for constructive criticism and use it as an opportunity for growth. By continuously learning and developing, you can enhance your job satisfaction and advance in your career.

Embracing New Challenges and Responsibilities

Embracing new challenges and responsibilities is crucial for job satisfaction. When individuals step out of their comfort zones and take on new tasks, they are more likely to feel a sense of accomplishment and fulfillment.

To embrace new challenges and responsibilities, be open to learning new skills and taking on additional responsibilities. Volunteer for projects or assignments that align with your interests and goals. Seek opportunities to expand your knowledge and expertise in your field.

It is also important to have a growth mindset and view challenges as opportunities for learning and growth. Embrace failures as learning experiences and use them to improve and develop.

Finding Meaning and Purpose in Your Work

Finding meaning and purpose in your work is essential for job satisfaction. When individuals feel that their work has a positive impact and aligns with their values, they are more likely to feel fulfilled and motivated.

To find meaning and purpose in your work, reflect on the impact that your work has on others. Consider how your skills and expertise contribute to the success of your organization or the well-being of others. Connect with the mission and values of your organization and find ways to align your work with them.

It is also important to set meaningful goals for yourself. Identify what you want to achieve in your career and how it can contribute to your personal growth and the greater good. By finding meaning and purpose in your work, you can enhance your job satisfaction and overall well-being.

Celebrating Your Achievements and Successes

Celebrating achievements and successes is crucial for job satisfaction. When individuals acknowledge their accomplishments, they are more likely to feel valued and motivated in their jobs.

To celebrate achievements and successes, take time to reflect on your accomplishments. Acknowledge the progress you have made and the goals you have achieved. Share your successes with others and express gratitude for their support.

It is also important to reward yourself for your hard work. Treat yourself to something special or engage in activities that bring you joy. By celebrating your achievements, you can enhance your job satisfaction and maintain a positive mindset.

Knowing When it's Time to Move On

Knowing when it's time to move on from a job is crucial for job satisfaction. Sometimes, despite our best efforts, we may find ourselves in a situation where our needs are not being met or where we no longer feel fulfilled.

Signs that it's time to move on include feeling consistently unhappy or unfulfilled in your job, experiencing high levels of stress or burnout, and having limited opportunities for growth and development. It is important to listen to your intuition and trust your instincts.

If you decide that it's time to make a career change, take the time to explore your options and identify what you want in your next job. Update your resume and reach out to your network for support and guidance. Consider seeking the help of a career coach or counselor who can provide insights and assistance in the job search process.

In conclusion, job satisfaction is a crucial aspect of our professional lives. It has a significant impact on our overall well-being, productivity, and engagement in our jobs. By understanding the importance of job satisfaction and taking steps to enhance it, we can create fulfilling and meaningful careers. Remember to set clear career goals, assess your current job satisfaction level, analyze the factors affecting your job satisfaction, build positive relationships at work, create a healthy work-life balance, seek professional development opportunities, embrace new challenges and responsibilities, find meaning and purpose in your work, celebrate achievements and successes, and know when it's time to move on. By prioritizing job satisfaction, you can create a fulfilling and rewarding career.

Chapter 4: The Future of Mentorship: How Technology is Changing the Landscape

Mentorship is a powerful tool that has been used for centuries to guide and support individuals in their personal and professional growth. It is a relationship in which a more experienced or knowledgeable person, known as the mentor, provides guidance, advice, and support to a less experienced or knowledgeable person, known as the mentee. Mentorship plays a crucial role in helping individuals navigate their careers, develop new skills, and achieve their goals.

In today's fast-paced and ever-changing world, mentorship is more important than ever. With the rapid advancements in technology and the increasing complexity of the global economy, individuals need guidance and support to navigate the challenges and opportunities that come their way. Mentorship provides a safe space for individuals to learn from someone who has been there before, to gain insights and perspectives that they may not have considered on their own.

The landscape of mentorship has also evolved over time. While traditional mentorship models have been effective in the past, they have their limitations and challenges. With the advent of technology, new opportunities for mentorship have emerged, disrupting traditional models and opening up new possibilities for mentorship in the digital age.

The Traditional Model of Mentorship: Limitations and Challenges

The traditional model of mentorship typically involves a one-on-one relationship between a mentor and a mentee. The mentor is usually someone who is more experienced or knowledgeable in a particular field or industry, while the mentee is someone who is seeking guidance and support to advance their career or develop new skills.

While this model has been effective in many cases, it has its limitations and challenges. One of the main limitations is that it relies on finding a suitable mentor who is willing and able to commit their time and energy to the mentoring relationship. This can be challenging, especially for individuals who are looking for mentors in niche industries or who are geographically isolated.

Another challenge is that traditional mentorship models often lack diversity and inclusivity. Many mentors tend to gravitate towards mentees who are similar to themselves in terms of background, experience, and interests. This can result in a lack of representation and opportunities for individuals from underrepresented groups.

Furthermore, traditional mentorship models can be time-consuming and resource-intensive. Mentors and mentees often have to meet in person or have regular phone calls, which can be difficult to schedule and coordinate, especially for busy professionals. This can limit the scalability and accessibility of mentorship programs.

How Technology is Disrupting Traditional Mentorship Models

Technology has revolutionized almost every aspect of our lives, and mentorship is no exception. The rise of digital platforms and tools has disrupted traditional mentorship models, opening up new possibilities for mentorship in the digital age.

One way technology is changing mentorship is through virtual mentorship platforms. These platforms connect mentors and mentees from around the world, breaking down geographical barriers and allowing individuals to find mentors who are a perfect fit for their needs. Virtual mentorship platforms also offer flexibility in terms of scheduling and communication, allowing mentors and mentees to connect at their own convenience.

Another way technology is disrupting traditional mentorship models is through the use of artificial intelligence (AI). AI-powered mentorship platforms can analyze data from multiple sources to provide personalized recommendations and insights to mentees. These platforms can also automate certain aspects of the mentoring process, such as scheduling meetings or tracking progress, freeing up mentors' time and energy.

Additionally, technology has enabled the use of big data in mentorship. By collecting and analyzing large amounts of data, mentors and mentees can gain valuable insights into trends, patterns, and best practices in their field. This data-driven approach can help mentees make more informed decisions and accelerate their learning and growth.

The Emergence of Virtual Mentorship Platforms: What You Need to Know

Virtual mentorship platforms have emerged as a popular and effective way to connect mentors and mentees in the digital age. These platforms leverage technology to facilitate mentorship relationships, offering a wide range of benefits and drawbacks.

One of the main benefits of virtual mentorship platforms is the ability to connect with mentors from around the world. These platforms allow mentees to find mentors who are a perfect fit for their needs, regardless of geographical location. This opens up a world of opportunities for individuals who may not have access to mentors in their local area or who are looking for mentors with specific expertise or experience.

Virtual mentorship platforms also offer flexibility in terms of scheduling and communication. Mentors and mentees can connect at their own convenience, using various communication tools such as video calls, instant messaging, or email. This flexibility makes mentorship more accessible and scalable, allowing mentors to support multiple mentees and mentees to seek guidance from multiple mentors.

However, virtual mentorship platforms also have their drawbacks. One of the main challenges is building trust and rapport in a virtual setting. Without the benefit of face-to-face interactions, it can be more difficult for mentors and mentees to establish a strong connection and build a meaningful relationship. This can impact the effectiveness of the mentorship experience.

Another challenge is the potential for miscommunication or misunderstanding in a virtual setting. Without the benefit of non-verbal cues, such as body language or facial expressions, it can be more difficult to convey emotions or intentions accurately. This can lead to misunderstandings or misinterpretations, which can hinder the mentorship process.

The Role of Artificial Intelligence in Mentorship: Opportunities and Risks

Artificial intelligence (AI) is playing an increasingly important role in mentorship, offering new opportunities and risks. AI-powered mentorship platforms can analyze data from multiple sources to provide personalized recommendations and insights to mentees. This data-driven approach can help mentees make more informed decisions and accelerate their learning and growth.

One of the main opportunities of AI-enabled mentorship is the ability to provide personalized recommendations and insights. AI algorithms can analyze data from multiple sources, such as the mentee's profile, past interactions, and external data sources, to understand their needs, preferences, and goals. Based on this analysis, the AI system can provide tailored recommendations and insights to help the mentee achieve their objectives.

Another opportunity of AI-enabled mentorship is the ability to automate certain aspects of the mentoring process. AI systems can handle routine tasks, such as scheduling meetings or tracking progress, freeing up mentors' time and energy to focus on more strategic or high-value activities. This can increase the scalability and efficiency of mentorship programs.

However, there are also risks associated with AI-enabled mentorship. One of the main risks is the potential for bias in AI algorithms. AI systems are only as good as the data they are trained on, and if the training data is biased or incomplete, it can lead to biased or inaccurate recommendations. This can perpetuate existing inequalities or reinforce stereotypes.

Another risk is the potential for over-reliance on AI systems. While AI can provide valuable insights and recommendations, it should not replace human judgment and intuition. Mentorship is a deeply human experience that requires empathy, emotional intelligence, and a deep understanding of individual needs and aspirations. It is important to strike a balance between leveraging AI technology and maintaining human connection in mentorship.

The Power of Big Data in Mentorship: Leveraging Analytics to Drive Results

Big data has emerged as a powerful tool in mentorship, allowing mentors and mentees to leverage analytics to drive results. By collecting and analyzing large amounts of data, mentors and mentees can gain valuable insights into trends, patterns, and best practices in their field.

One of the main benefits of using big data in mentorship is the ability to identify trends and patterns. By analyzing data from multiple sources, such as industry reports, market research, or social media, mentors and mentees can gain a deeper understanding of the current landscape and anticipate future developments. This can help mentees make more informed decisions and stay ahead of the curve.

Another benefit of using big data in mentorship is the ability to benchmark performance. By comparing their own performance against industry standards or best practices, mentees can identify areas for improvement and set realistic goals. This data-driven approach can help mentees track their progress and measure their success.

However, there are also drawbacks to using big data in mentorship. One of the main challenges is the potential for information overload. With access to vast amounts of data, it can be overwhelming for mentors and mentees to filter through the noise and identify the most relevant and actionable insights. It is important to have a clear strategy and framework for collecting, analyzing, and interpreting data in mentorship.

Another challenge is the potential for privacy and security concerns. Big data often involves collecting and analyzing personal or sensitive information, such as performance metrics or feedback. It is important to ensure that proper safeguards are in place to protect individuals' privacy and comply with relevant regulations.

The Rise of Social Media and Peer-to-Peer Mentorship: Benefits and Drawbacks

Social media has transformed the way we connect, communicate, and learn from each other, including in the context of mentorship. The rise of social media has given rise to peer-to-peer mentorship, where individuals can learn from their peers who have similar interests or experiences.

One of the main benefits of peer-to-peer mentorship through social media is the ability to connect with a diverse range of individuals from around the world. Social media platforms allow individuals to find like-minded peers who share similar interests or goals, regardless of geographical location. This opens up a world of opportunities for individuals to learn from each other and gain new perspectives.

Another benefit of peer-to-peer mentorship through social media is the ability to access real-time information and insights. Social media platforms are constantly updated with the latest news, trends, and best practices, allowing individuals to stay informed and up-to-date. This can help mentees make more informed decisions and adapt to changing circumstances.

However, there are also drawbacks to peer-to-peer mentorship through social media. One of the main challenges is the potential for misinformation or inaccurate information. Social media platforms are often filled with opinions, rumors, or unverified claims, which can be misleading or harmful. It is important for individuals to critically evaluate the information they come across and seek reliable sources.

Another challenge is the potential for superficial or shallow connections. Social media platforms often prioritize quantity over quality, with individuals accumulating a large number of followers or connections. This can lead to superficial interactions or a lack of meaningful engagement. It is important for individuals to cultivate genuine relationships and invest time and effort in building meaningful connections.

Virtual Reality and Augmented Reality: Transforming the Future of Mentorship

Virtual reality (VR) and augmented reality (AR) are emerging technologies that have the potential to transform the future of mentorship. VR allows individuals to immerse themselves in a virtual environment, while AR overlays digital information onto the real world.

One of the main benefits of VR and AR-enabled mentorship is the ability to provide immersive and interactive learning experiences. VR can simulate real-world scenarios, allowing mentees to practice skills or solve problems in a safe and controlled environment. AR can provide real-time guidance or information, enhancing mentees' understanding and performance.

Another benefit of VR and AR-enabled mentorship is the ability to overcome geographical barriers. VR and AR technologies can connect mentors and mentees from around the world, allowing them to interact as if they were in the same physical space. This opens up new possibilities for mentorship, especially for individuals who are geographically isolated or who have limited access to mentors in their local area.

However, there are also drawbacks to VR and AR-enabled mentorship. One of the main challenges is the cost and accessibility of the technology. VR and AR devices can be expensive, making them inaccessible to individuals with limited financial resources. It is important to ensure that these technologies are affordable and accessible to all individuals who can benefit from them.

Another challenge is the potential for sensory overload or discomfort. VR and AR experiences can be intense and overwhelming, especially for individuals who are not accustomed to these technologies. It is important to provide proper training and support to mentees to ensure a positive and comfortable experience.

The Importance of Soft Skills in the Age of Digital Mentorship

In the age of digital mentorship, soft skills play a crucial role in building meaningful connections and driving success. Soft skills are personal attributes that enable individuals to interact effectively and harmoniously with others, such as communication, empathy, or problem-solving.

One of the main reasons why soft skills are important in digital mentorship is the need for effective communication. In a virtual setting, where face-to-face interactions are limited, it is important for mentors and mentees to be able to communicate clearly and effectively through written or verbal communication. This includes being able to express ideas, ask questions, or provide feedback in a concise and respectful manner.

Another reason why soft skills are important in digital mentorship is the need for empathy and emotional intelligence. In a virtual setting, where non-verbal cues are limited, it can be more difficult to understand others' emotions or intentions. It is important for mentors and mentees to be able to empathize with each other, understand each other's perspectives, and build trust and rapport.

Furthermore, soft skills such as problem-solving or critical thinking are essential in digital mentorship. In a rapidly changing and complex world, mentors and mentees need to be able to adapt to new challenges, think creatively, and find innovative solutions. Soft skills enable individuals to approach problems with a growth mindset, embrace uncertainty, and learn from failures.

The Ethics of Technology-Enabled Mentorship: Balancing Human Connection and Automation

As technology continues to advance, it is important to consider the ethical implications of technology-enabled mentorship. Balancing human connection and automation is crucial to ensure that mentorship remains a meaningful and impactful experience.

One of the main ethical considerations in technology-enabled mentorship is the potential for bias in AI algorithms. AI systems are only as good as the data they are trained on, and if the training data is biased or incomplete, it can lead to biased or inaccurate recommendations. This can perpetuate existing inequalities or reinforce stereotypes. It is important to ensure that AI algorithms are transparent, accountable, and fair.

Another ethical consideration is the potential for privacy and security concerns. Technology-enabled mentorship often involves collecting and analyzing personal or sensitive information, such as performance metrics or feedback. It is important to ensure that proper safeguards are in place to protect individuals' privacy and comply with relevant regulations. This includes obtaining informed consent, anonymizing data when possible, and implementing robust security measures.

Furthermore, it is important to strike a balance between leveraging technology and maintaining human connection in mentorship. While AI can provide valuable insights and recommendations, it should not replace human judgment and intuition. Mentorship is a deeply human experience that requires empathy, emotional intelligence , and the ability to understand and respond to the unique needs and challenges of each mentee. These qualities cannot be replicated by technology alone. Additionally, human connection is essential for building trust and fostering a supportive environment in which mentees feel comfortable sharing their goals, fears, and aspirations. Technology can enhance mentorship by facilitating communication, providing access to resources, and streamlining administrative tasks, but it should always be used as a tool to augment the mentor-mentee relationship rather than replace it. Ultimately, the most effective mentorship experiences are those that combine the power of technology with the warmth and understanding that only a human mentor can provide.

Chapter 5: The Power of Perseverance: Real-Life Success Stories

Perseverance is defined as the ability to persist in the face of challenges, obstacles, and setbacks. It is the determination to keep going, even when things get tough. Perseverance is a crucial trait to possess if one wants to achieve success in any area of life. Without it, it is easy to give up when faced with difficulties or setbacks. However, with perseverance, one can overcome adversity and achieve their goals.

Perseverance is important in achieving success because it allows individuals to push through obstacles and setbacks that may arise along their journey. It helps them stay focused on their goals and not get discouraged by temporary failures. Perseverance also builds resilience and mental strength, which are essential qualities for success. It teaches individuals to keep going even when things seem impossible, and to never give up on their dreams.

Overcoming Adversity: The Inspiring Story of Oprah Winfrey

Oprah Winfrey is a prime example of someone who has overcome adversity through perseverance. Born into poverty in rural Mississippi, Oprah faced numerous challenges throughout her childhood. She was raised by her grandmother and endured physical and emotional abuse. Despite these difficult circumstances, Oprah was determined to create a better life for herself.

Through hard work and perseverance, Oprah rose to become one of the most successful media moguls in the world. She started her career as a radio host and eventually became the host of her own talk show, "The Oprah Winfrey Show," which became the highest-rated television program of its kind. Oprah's story is a testament to the power of perseverance and the ability to overcome adversity.

From Homeless to Billionaire: The Tenacity of J.K. Rowling

J.K. Rowling's journey to success is another inspiring story of perseverance. Before she became a household name as the author of the Harry Potter series, Rowling faced numerous struggles and setbacks. She was a single mother living on welfare and battling depression. Despite these challenges, Rowling never gave up on her dream of becoming a writer.

Rowling's perseverance paid off when she finally finished writing the first Harry Potter book. However, her journey to getting it published was not easy. She faced rejection from multiple publishers before finally finding one who believed in her work. The success of the Harry Potter franchise is a testament to Rowling's perseverance and the power of never giving up on one's dreams.

The Power of Persistence: How Thomas Edison Failed His Way to Success

Thomas Edison is often credited with inventing the light bulb, but his path to success was filled with failures and setbacks. Edison made numerous attempts at inventing a practical incandescent light bulb, but each attempt ended in failure. Despite these setbacks, Edison never gave up on his goal.

Edison's perseverance eventually paid off when he finally invented a commercially viable light bulb after thousands of failed attempts.

His determination and refusal to give up are what led to his eventual success. Edison's story is a powerful reminder that failure is not the end, but rather an opportunity to learn and grow.

Never Giving Up: The Story of Michael Jordan's Rise to NBA Greatness

Michael Jordan is widely regarded as one of the greatest basketball players of all time, but his journey to greatness was not without its challenges. As a young player, Jordan faced numerous setbacks and failures. He was cut from his high school basketball team, which only fueled his determination to prove himself.

Jordan's perseverance and relentless work ethic allowed him to improve his skills and eventually become a star player in college and the NBA. He went on to win six NBA championships and earn numerous accolades throughout his career. Jordan's story is a testament to the power of perseverance and the importance of never giving up on one's dreams.

The Unbreakable Spirit of Nelson Mandela: A Story of Perseverance and Triumph

Nelson Mandela's story is one of the most inspiring examples of perseverance in the face of adversity. Mandela spent 27 years in prison for his fight against apartheid in South Africa. Despite the harsh conditions and long years of imprisonment, Mandela never lost hope or gave up on his fight for equality and justice.

Mandela's perseverance eventually paid off when he was released from prison and went on to become South Africa's first black president. His unwavering determination and commitment to his cause are what led to the end of apartheid and the establishment of a democratic South Africa. Mandela's story serves as a reminder that perseverance can lead to triumph, even in the face of seemingly insurmountable odds.

The Long Road to Victory: The Inspiring Story of Serena Williams

Serena Williams is widely regarded as one of the greatest tennis players of all time, but her journey to success was not without its challenges. As a young player, Serena faced racism and discrimination in the tennis world. She also struggled with self-doubt and injuries throughout her career.

Despite these challenges, Serena never gave up on her dream of becoming a champion. She persevered through countless hours of training and hard work, constantly pushing herself to improve her game. Serena went on to win 23 Grand Slam singles titles and become an inspiration to aspiring athletes around the world. Her story is a testament to the power of perseverance and the importance of never giving up on one's dreams.

The Power of Belief: How Arnold Schwarzenegger Became a Hollywood Legend

Arnold Schwarzenegger's journey from a small town in Austria to becoming a Hollywood legend is a story of perseverance and determination. When Schwarzenegger first arrived in America, he faced numerous challenges as an immigrant. He struggled with the English language and faced criticism for his thick accent and unconventional physique.

However, Schwarzenegger never let these challenges deter him from pursuing his dreams. He persevered through years of bodybuilding competitions, eventually becoming a seven-time Mr. Olympia champion. Schwarzenegger then transitioned into acting, where he faced even more skepticism and rejection. But through hard work and perseverance, he went on to become one of the biggest action stars in Hollywood. Schwarzenegger's story is a testament to the power of belief in oneself and the importance of never giving up on one's dreams.

From Refugee to Supermodel: The Incredible Journey of Iman

Iman's journey from Somalia to becoming a supermodel and businesswoman is a story of perseverance and resilience. As a young girl, Iman fled war-torn Somalia with her family and sought refuge in Kenya. Despite the hardships she faced as a refugee, Iman never lost sight of her dreams.

Iman's perseverance paid off when she was discovered by a photographer while attending university in Nairobi. She went on to become one of the most successful supermodels of her time, gracing the covers of numerous fashion magazines and walking the runways for top designers. In addition to her modeling career, Iman also launched her own cosmetics line and became a successful businesswoman. Her story is a testament to the power of perseverance and the ability to overcome adversity.

The Courage to Keep Going: The Story of Malala Yousafzai

Malala Yousafzai's fight for education in Pakistan is an inspiring example of perseverance in the face of danger and adversity. Malala was just 15 years old when she was shot by the Taliban for advocating for girls' education. Despite this horrific attack, Malala refused to be silenced.

Malala's perseverance and courage led her to become an international advocate for education and the youngest-ever Nobel Peace Prize laureate. She continues to fight for the rights of girls to receive an education and has become a symbol of hope and resilience for millions around the world. Malala's story is a powerful reminder that even in the face of great danger, perseverance can lead to positive change.

The Importance of Perseverance in Achieving Your Dreams.

The stories of perseverance shared above serve as powerful reminders of the importance of never giving up on one's dreams. Perseverance is a crucial trait to possess if one wants to achieve success in any area of life. It allows individuals to push through obstacles, setbacks, and failures, and stay focused on their goals.

Perseverance builds resilience, mental strength, and determination. It teaches individuals to keep going even when things seem impossible and to never give up on their dreams. The stories of Oprah Winfrey, J.K. Rowling, Thomas Edison, Michael Jordan, Nelson Mandela,

Serena Williams, Arnold Schwarzenegger, Iman, and Malala Yousafzai are all testament to the power of perseverance.

So, if you find yourself facing challenges or setbacks on your journey towards success, remember these stories and let them inspire you to keep going. Persevere through the tough times, stay focused on your goals, and never give up on your dreams. With perseverance, anything is possible.

Chapter 6: The Future of Mentorship

Mentorship is a powerful tool that has been used for centuries to guide and support individuals in their personal and professional growth. It is a relationship in which a more experienced or knowledgeable person, known as the mentor, provides guidance, advice, and support to a less experienced or knowledgeable person, known as the mentee. Mentorship plays a crucial role in helping individuals navigate their careers, develop new skills, and achieve their goals.

In today's fast-paced and ever-changing world, mentorship is more important than ever. With the rapid advancements in technology and the increasing complexity of the global economy, individuals need guidance and support to navigate the challenges and opportunities that come their way. Mentorship provides a safe space for individuals to learn from someone who has been there before, to gain insights and perspectives that they may not have considered on their own.

The landscape of mentorship has also evolved over time. While traditional mentorship models have been effective in the past, they have their limitations and challenges. With the advent of technology, new opportunities for mentorship have emerged, disrupting traditional models and opening up new possibilities for mentorship in the digital age.

The Traditional Model of Mentorship: Limitations and Challenges

The traditional model of mentorship typically involves a one-on-one relationship between a mentor and a mentee. The mentor is usually someone who is more experienced or knowledgeable in a particular field or industry, while the mentee is someone who is seeking guidance and support to advance their career or develop new skills.

While this model has been effective in many cases, it has its limitations and challenges. One of the main limitations is that it relies on finding a suitable mentor who is willing and able to commit their time and energy to the mentoring relationship. This can be challenging, especially for individuals who are looking for mentors in niche industries or who are geographically isolated.

Another challenge is that traditional mentorship models often lack diversity and inclusivity. Many mentors tend to gravitate towards mentees who are similar to themselves in terms of background, experience, and interests. This can result in a lack of representation and opportunities for individuals from underrepresented groups.

Furthermore, traditional mentorship models can be time-consuming and resource-intensive. Mentors and mentees often have to meet in person or have regular phone calls, which can be difficult to schedule and coordinate, especially for busy professionals. This can limit the scalability and accessibility of mentorship programs.

How Technology is Disrupting Traditional Mentorship Models

Technology has revolutionized almost every aspect of our lives, and mentorship is no exception. The rise of digital platforms and tools has disrupted traditional mentorship models, opening up new possibilities for mentorship in the digital age.

One way technology is changing mentorship is through virtual mentorship platforms. These platforms connect mentors and mentees from around the world, breaking down geographical barriers and allowing individuals to find mentors who are a perfect fit for their needs. Virtual mentorship platforms also offer flexibility in terms of scheduling and communication, allowing mentors and mentees to connect at their own convenience.

Another way technology is disrupting traditional mentorship models is through the use of artificial intelligence (AI). AI-powered mentorship platforms can analyze data from multiple sources to provide personalized recommendations and insights to mentees. These platforms can also automate certain aspects of the mentoring process, such as scheduling meetings or tracking progress, freeing up mentors' time and energy.

Additionally, technology has enabled the use of big data in mentorship. By collecting and analyzing large amounts of data, mentors and mentees can gain valuable insights into trends, patterns, and best practices in their field. This data-driven approach can help mentees make more informed decisions and accelerate their learning and growth.

The Emergence of Virtual Mentorship Platforms: What You Need to Know

Virtual mentorship platforms have emerged as a popular and effective way to connect mentors and mentees in the digital age. These platforms leverage technology to facilitate mentorship relationships, offering a wide range of benefits and drawbacks.

One of the main benefits of virtual mentorship platforms is the ability to connect with mentors from around the world. These platforms allow mentees to find mentors who are a perfect fit for their needs, regardless of geographical location. This opens up a world of opportunities for individuals who may not have access to mentors in their local area or who are looking for mentors with specific expertise or experience.

Virtual mentorship platforms also offer flexibility in terms of scheduling and communication. Mentors and mentees can connect at their own convenience, using various communication tools such as video calls, instant messaging, or email. This flexibility makes mentorship more accessible and scalable, allowing mentors to support multiple mentees and mentees to seek guidance from multiple mentors.

However, virtual mentorship platforms also have their drawbacks. One of the main challenges is building trust and rapport in a virtual setting. Without the benefit of face-to-face interactions, it can be more difficult for mentors and mentees to establish a strong connection and build a meaningful relationship. This can impact the effectiveness of the mentorship experience.

Another challenge is the potential for miscommunication or misunderstanding in a virtual setting. Without the benefit of non-verbal cues, such as body language or facial expressions, it can be more difficult to convey emotions or intentions accurately. This can lead to misunderstandings or misinterpretations, which can hinder the mentorship process.

The Role of Artificial Intelligence in Mentorship: Opportunities and Risks

Artificial intelligence (AI) is playing an increasingly important role in mentorship, offering new opportunities and risks. AI-powered mentorship platforms can analyze data from multiple sources to provide personalized recommendations and insights to mentees. This data-driven approach can help mentees make more informed decisions and accelerate their learning and growth.

One of the main opportunities of AI-enabled mentorship is the ability to provide personalized recommendations and insights. AI algorithms can analyze data from multiple sources, such as the mentee's profile, past interactions, and external data sources, to understand their needs, preferences, and goals. Based on this analysis, the AI system can provide tailored recommendations and insights to help the mentee achieve their objectives.

Another opportunity of AI-enabled mentorship is the ability to automate certain aspects of the mentoring process. AI systems can handle routine tasks, such as scheduling meetings or tracking progress, freeing up mentors' time and energy to focus on more strategic or high-value activities. This can increase the scalability and efficiency of mentorship programs.

However, there are also risks associated with AI-enabled mentorship. One of the main risks is the potential for bias in AI algorithms. AI systems are only as good as the data they are trained on, and if the training data is biased or incomplete, it can lead to biased or inaccurate recommendations. This can perpetuate existing inequalities or reinforce stereotypes.

Another risk is the potential for over-reliance on AI systems. While AI can provide valuable insights and recommendations, it should not replace human judgment and intuition. Mentorship is a deeply human experience that requires empathy, emotional intelligence, and a deep understanding of individual needs and aspirations. It is important to strike a balance between leveraging AI technology and maintaining human connection in mentorship.

The Power of Big Data in Mentorship: Leveraging Analytics to Drive Results

Big data has emerged as a powerful tool in mentorship, allowing mentors and mentees to leverage analytics to drive results. By collecting and analyzing large amounts of data, mentors and mentees can gain valuable insights into trends, patterns, and best practices in their field.

One of the main benefits of using big data in mentorship is the ability to identify trends and patterns. By analyzing data from multiple sources, such as industry reports, market research, or social media, mentors and mentees can gain a deeper understanding of the current landscape and anticipate future developments. This can help mentees make more informed decisions and stay ahead of the curve.

Another benefit of using big data in mentorship is the ability to benchmark performance. By comparing their own performance against industry standards or best practices, mentees can identify areas for improvement and set realistic goals. This data-driven approach can help mentees track their progress and measure their success.

However, there are also drawbacks to using big data in mentorship. One of the main challenges is the potential for information overload. With access to vast amounts of data, it can be overwhelming for mentors and mentees to filter through the noise and identify the most relevant and actionable insights. It is important to have a clear strategy and framework for collecting, analyzing, and interpreting data in mentorship.

Another challenge is the potential for privacy and security concerns. Big data often involves collecting and analyzing personal or sensitive information, such as performance metrics or feedback. It is important to ensure that proper safeguards are in place to protect individuals' privacy and comply with relevant regulations.

The Rise of Social Media and Peer-to-Peer Mentorship: Benefits and Drawbacks

Social media has transformed the way we connect, communicate, and learn from each other, including in the context of mentorship. The rise of social media has given rise to peer-to-peer mentorship, where individuals can learn from their peers who have similar interests or experiences.

One of the main benefits of peer-to-peer mentorship through social media is the ability to connect with a diverse range of individuals from around the world. Social media platforms allow individuals to find like-minded peers who share similar interests or goals, regardless of geographical location. This opens up a world of opportunities for individuals to learn from each other and gain new perspectives.

Another benefit of peer-to-peer mentorship through social media is the ability to access real-time information and insights. Social media platforms are constantly updated with the latest news, trends, and best practices, allowing individuals to stay informed and up-to-date. This can help mentees make more informed decisions and adapt to changing circumstances.

However, there are also drawbacks to peer-to-peer mentorship through social media. One of the main challenges is the potential for misinformation or inaccurate information. Social media platforms are often filled with opinions, rumors, or unverified claims, which can be misleading or harmful. It is important for individuals to critically evaluate the information they come across and seek reliable sources.

Another challenge is the potential for superficial or shallow connections. Social media platforms often prioritize quantity over quality, with individuals accumulating a large number of followers or connections. This can lead to superficial interactions or a lack of meaningful engagement. It is important for individuals to cultivate genuine relationships and invest time and effort in building meaningful connections.

Virtual Reality and Augmented Reality: Transforming the Future of Mentorship

Virtual reality (VR) and augmented reality (AR) are emerging technologies that have the potential to transform the future of mentorship. VR allows individuals to immerse themselves in a virtual environment, while AR overlays digital information onto the real world.

One of the main benefits of VR and AR-enabled mentorship is the ability to provide immersive and interactive learning experiences. VR can simulate real-world scenarios, allowing mentees to practice skills or solve problems in a safe and controlled environment. AR can provide real-time guidance or information, enhancing mentees' understanding and performance.

Another benefit of VR and AR-enabled mentorship is the ability to overcome geographical barriers. VR and AR technologies can connect mentors and mentees from around the world, allowing them to interact as if they were in the same physical space. This opens up new possibilities for mentorship, especially for individuals who are geographically isolated or who have limited access to mentors in their local area.

However, there are also drawbacks to VR and AR-enabled mentorship. One of the main challenges is the cost and accessibility of the technology. VR and AR devices can be expensive, making them inaccessible to individuals with limited financial resources. It is important to ensure that these technologies are affordable and accessible to all individuals who can benefit from them.

Another challenge is the potential for sensory overload or discomfort. VR and AR experiences can be intense and overwhelming, especially for individuals who are not accustomed to these technologies. It is important to provide proper training and support to mentees to ensure a positive and comfortable experience.

The Importance of Soft Skills in the Age of Digital Mentorship

In the age of digital mentorship, soft skills play a crucial role in building meaningful connections and driving success. Soft skills are personal attributes that enable individuals to interact effectively and harmoniously with others, such as communication, empathy, or problem-solving.

One of the main reasons why soft skills are important in digital mentorship is the need for effective communication. In a virtual setting, where face-to-face interactions are limited, it is important for mentors and mentees to be able to communicate clearly and effectively through written or verbal communication. This includes being able to express ideas, ask questions, or provide feedback in a concise and respectful manner.

Another reason why soft skills are important in digital mentorship is the need for empathy and emotional intelligence. In a virtual setting, where non-verbal cues are limited, it can be more difficult to understand others' emotions or intentions. It is important for mentors and mentees to be able to empathize with each other, understand each other's perspectives, and build trust and rapport.

Furthermore, soft skills such as problem-solving or critical thinking are essential in digital mentorship. In a rapidly changing and complex world, mentors and mentees need to be able to adapt to new challenges, think creatively, and find innovative solutions. Soft skills enable individuals to approach problems with a growth mindset, embrace uncertainty, and learn from failures.

The Ethics of Technology-Enabled Mentorship: Balancing Human Connection and Automation

As technology continues to advance, it is important to consider the ethical implications of technology-enabled mentorship. Balancing human connection and automation is crucial to ensure that mentorship remains a meaningful and impactful experience.

One of the main ethical considerations in technology-enabled mentorship is the potential for bias in AI algorithms. AI systems are only as good as the data they are trained on, and if the training data is biased or incomplete, it can lead to biased or inaccurate recommendations. This can perpetuate existing inequalities or reinforce stereotypes. It is important to ensure that AI algorithms are transparent, accountable, and fair.

Another ethical consideration is the potential for privacy and security concerns. Technology-enabled mentorship often involves collecting and analyzing personal or sensitive information, such as performance metrics or feedback. It is important to ensure that proper safeguards are in place to protect individuals' privacy and comply with relevant regulations. This includes obtaining informed consent, anonymizing data when possible, and implementing robust security measures.

Furthermore, it is important to strike a balance between leveraging technology and maintaining human connection in mentorship. While AI can provide valuable insights and recommendations, it should not replace human judgment and intuition. Mentorship is a deeply human experience that requires empathy, emotional intelligence , and the ability to understand and respond to the unique needs and challenges of each mentee. These qualities cannot be replicated by technology alone. Additionally, human connection is essential for building trust and fostering a supportive environment in which mentees feel comfortable sharing their goals, fears, and aspirations. Technology can enhance mentorship by facilitating communication, providing access to resources, and streamlining administrative tasks, but it should always be used as a tool to augment the mentor-mentee relationship rather than replace it. Ultimately, the most effective mentorship experiences are those that combine the power of technology with the warmth and understanding that only a human mentor can provide.

Chapter 7: The Science of Learning

The field of learning science is a multidisciplinary field that combines principles from psychology, neuroscience, and education to understand how people learn and how to optimize the learning process. It seeks to answer questions such as: What are the most effective teaching methods? How can we enhance memory retention? What motivates learners to engage in the learning process? By studying the science of learning, we can gain valuable insights into how to design and deliver effective training programs.

Understanding how people learn is crucial for the development of effective training programs. Without this understanding, training programs may fail to engage learners or may not effectively transfer knowledge and skills. By applying the principles of learning science, trainers can create programs that are tailored to the needs of learners, resulting in improved learning outcomes.

The Psychology of Effective Training

Effective training programs are grounded in principles of psychology that take into account the learner's perspective. One key principle is that learners are more likely to engage and retain information when they perceive it as relevant and meaningful. Therefore, trainers should strive to make connections between the content being taught and real-world applications or personal experiences.

Another important principle is that learners have different levels of prior knowledge and experience. Trainers should consider this when designing training programs and provide opportunities for learners to build on their existing knowledge. This can be done through pre-assessments or by incorporating activities that allow learners to reflect on their prior knowledge.

Understanding the Learning Process

The learning process can be divided into several stages: acquisition, consolidation, and retrieval. During the acquisition stage, learners are exposed to new information or skills. This stage is characterized by active engagement with the material, such as reading, listening, or observing.

The consolidation stage is when learners process and integrate the new information into their existing knowledge structures. This stage is crucial for long-term retention and involves activities such as reflection, summarization, or practice.

The retrieval stage is when learners recall and apply the information or skills they have learned. This stage is important for reinforcing learning and transferring knowledge to new contexts. Trainers should be aware of these stages and design activities that support each stage of the learning process.

The Role of Memory in Learning

Memory plays a crucial role in the learning process. There are several types of memory, including sensory memory, short-term memory, and long-term memory. Sensory memory holds information from our senses for a very brief period of time, while short-term memory allows us to hold a limited amount of information for a short period of time.

Long-term memory is where information is stored for an extended period of time. It can be further divided into declarative memory (which includes facts and events) and procedural memory (which includes skills and habits). Trainers should consider the limitations of working memory and the importance of repetition and practice in transferring information from short-term to long-term memory.

The Importance of Feedback in Learning

Feedback is an essential component of the learning process. It provides learners with information about their performance and helps them identify areas for improvement. There are different types of feedback, including corrective feedback (which points out errors and provides guidance on how to correct them) and positive feedback (which reinforces correct responses).

Timely and specific feedback is particularly important for effective learning. It allows learners to make immediate adjustments and reinforces correct responses or behaviors. Trainers should provide feedback that is clear, specific, and actionable, and should also encourage learners to reflect on their own performance.

Motivation and Learning: How to Keep Learners Engaged

Motivation plays a crucial role in the learning process. Learners who are motivated are more likely to engage in the learning process, persist in the face of challenges, and achieve better learning outcomes. There are different types of motivation, including intrinsic motivation (which comes from within the learner) and extrinsic motivation (which comes from external rewards or punishments).

Creating a motivating learning environment involves providing learners with autonomy, competence, and relatedness. Autonomy allows learners to have control over their learning process and make choices about what and how they learn. Competence involves providing learners with opportunities to develop and demonstrate their skills. Relatedness involves creating a sense of belonging and connection with others in the learning community.

The Power of Visualization in Learning

Visualization is a powerful tool that can aid in the learning process. It involves creating mental images or representations of information or concepts. Visualization can help learners make connections between different pieces of information, enhance memory retention, and improve understanding.

Incorporating visualization techniques in training programs can be done through the use of visual aids, such as diagrams, charts, or videos. Trainers can also encourage learners to create their own mental images or use guided imagery exercises to enhance visualization skills.

The Impact of Emotions on Learning

Emotions play a significant role in the learning process. Positive emotions, such as curiosity, interest, and enjoyment, can enhance motivation, attention, and memory. On the other hand, negative emotions, such as anxiety or boredom, can hinder learning by impairing attention and memory.

Creating a positive emotional environment for learning involves fostering a sense of safety and belonging, providing opportunities for success and mastery, and promoting a growth mindset. Trainers should be aware of the emotional states of learners and strive to create a supportive and positive learning environment.

Different Learning Styles: How to Cater to Individual Needs

Individuals have different learning styles, or preferences for how they process information. Some learners may prefer visual information, while others may prefer auditory or kinesthetic information. Recognizing and catering to individual learning styles can enhance engagement and understanding.

Trainers can incorporate different modalities of instruction to cater to different learning styles. For example, visual learners may benefit from the use of visual aids, while auditory learners may benefit from lectures or discussions. Kinesthetic learners may benefit from hands-on activities or simulations. Providing options and flexibility in the learning process can accommodate different learning styles.

The Science of Practice: How to Master Skills

Practice is a key component of skill acquisition and mastery. The science of practice, also known as deliberate practice, involves engaging in focused and structured practice activities that target specific skills or knowledge areas. Deliberate practice involves setting specific goals, receiving feedback, and engaging in repetitive and challenging activities.

Incorporating deliberate practice in training programs involves providing learners with opportunities to engage in targeted practice activities, receive feedback, and reflect on their performance. Trainers should also encourage learners to set specific goals and provide guidance on how to structure their practice sessions.

Applying the Science of Learning: Tips for Effective Training Programs

To create effective training programs, trainers should incorporate the principles of learning science into their design and delivery. Some practical tips include:

1. Make the content relevant and meaningful: Connect the material being taught to real-world applications or personal experiences to enhance engagement and understanding.

2. Consider the learner's perspective: Take into account learners' prior knowledge and experience and provide opportunities for reflection and building on existing knowledge.

3. Support the different stages of the learning process: Design activities that support acquisition, consolidation, and retrieval of information or skills.

4. Provide timely and specific feedback: Give feedback that is clear, specific, and actionable to help learners make immediate adjustments and reinforce correct responses.

5. Create a motivating learning environment: Foster autonomy, competence, and relatedness to enhance motivation and engagement.

6. Incorporate visualization techniques: Use visual aids or guided imagery exercises to enhance visualization skills and aid in understanding.

7. Foster a positive emotional environment: Create a sense of safety and belonging, provide opportunities for success and mastery, and promote a growth mindset.

8. Cater to individual learning styles: Provide options and flexibility in the learning process to accommodate different learning preferences.

9. Incorporate deliberate practice: Provide opportunities for focused and structured practice activities that target specific skills or knowledge areas.

10. Continuously evaluate and improve training programs: Regularly assess the effectiveness of training programs and make adjustments based on feedback and evaluation data.

Conclusion:

Understanding the science of learning is crucial for the development of effective training programs. By incorporating principles from psychology, neuroscience, and education, trainers can create programs that engage learners, optimize memory retention, and enhance motivation. By considering the learner's perspective, recognizing the different stages of the learning process, and catering to individual needs, trainers can create a supportive and effective learning environment. By applying the principles of learning science and continuously evaluating and improving training programs, we can ensure that learners are equipped with the knowledge and skills they need to succeed.

Chapter 8: How to Boost Your Job Satisfaction

Job satisfaction is a crucial aspect of our professional lives. It refers to the level of contentment and fulfillment that individuals experience in their jobs. When employees are satisfied with their work, they are more likely to be engaged, motivated, and productive. Job satisfaction also has a significant impact on overall well-being and mental health. In this article, we will explore the importance of job satisfaction and provide tips on how to enhance it.

Understanding the Importance of Job Satisfaction

Job satisfaction is defined as the positive emotional state resulting from an individual's appraisal of their job or job experiences. It encompasses various factors such as the nature of work, relationships with colleagues and superiors, compensation, and opportunities for growth and development.

When employees are satisfied with their jobs, they are more likely to be committed to their organizations and have higher levels of productivity. They are also more likely to experience lower levels of stress and burnout. Job satisfaction has been linked to increased job performance, reduced turnover rates, and improved overall well-being.

On the other hand, job dissatisfaction can have detrimental effects on both individuals and organizations. Employees who are dissatisfied with their jobs may experience decreased motivation, lower productivity, and higher rates of absenteeism. They may also be more prone to physical and mental health issues such as anxiety and depression.

Identifying Your Career Goals

Setting clear career goals is essential for job satisfaction. When individuals have a sense of direction and purpose in their careers, they are more likely to feel fulfilled and motivated in their work.

To identify your career goals, start by reflecting on your interests, values, and skills. Consider what you enjoy doing and what you are passionate about. Think about your long-term aspirations and where you see yourself in the future. It can also be helpful to seek guidance from mentors or career counselors who can provide insights and support in the goal-setting process.

Assessing Your Current Job Satisfaction Level

Assessing your current job satisfaction level is crucial for understanding what aspects of your job are contributing to your satisfaction or dissatisfaction. By identifying areas of improvement, you can take steps to enhance your job satisfaction.

There are various methods for assessing job satisfaction. One common approach is to use surveys or questionnaires that measure different dimensions of job satisfaction, such as work-life balance, compensation, and opportunities for growth. Another method is to engage in self-reflection and journaling to explore your feelings and thoughts about your job.

Analyzing the Factors Affecting Your Job Satisfaction

Several factors can influence job satisfaction. By analyzing these factors, you can gain insights into what aspects of your job are contributing to your satisfaction or dissatisfaction.

Common factors affecting job satisfaction include the nature of work, relationships with colleagues and superiors, compensation and benefits, work-life balance, and opportunities for growth and development. It is essential to assess each of these factors and determine which ones are most important to you.

To analyze the factors affecting your job satisfaction, consider keeping a journal where you can reflect on your experiences at work. Take note of the tasks that bring you joy and fulfillment, as well as the ones that drain your energy. Pay attention to the relationships you have with your colleagues and superiors and how they impact your overall satisfaction.

Building Positive Relationships with Colleagues and Superiors

Positive relationships at work play a significant role in job satisfaction. When individuals have supportive and collaborative relationships with their colleagues and superiors, they are more likely to feel valued and motivated in their jobs.

To build positive relationships at work, start by being respectful and considerate towards your colleagues and superiors. Show appreciation for their contributions and offer support when needed. Foster open communication by actively listening to others and expressing your thoughts and ideas clearly.

It is also important to be a team player and collaborate effectively with others. By working together towards common goals, you can create a positive and supportive work environment.

Creating a Healthy Work-Life Balance

Achieving a healthy work-life balance is crucial for job satisfaction. When individuals have time for their personal lives and hobbies, they are more likely to feel fulfilled and satisfied in their jobs.

To create a healthy work-life balance, set boundaries between your work and personal life. Establish specific times for work and leisure activities and stick to them as much as possible. Prioritize self-care by engaging in activities that help you relax and recharge.

It is also important to communicate your needs and expectations with your colleagues and superiors. Let them know when you need time off or when you are feeling overwhelmed. By advocating for yourself, you can create a work environment that supports your well-being.

Seeking Professional Development Opportunities

Professional development is essential for job satisfaction. When individuals have opportunities to learn and grow in their careers, they are more likely to feel engaged and motivated in their work.

To seek professional development opportunities, start by identifying your areas of interest and areas for improvement. Consider attending workshops, conferences, or seminars related to your field.

Take advantage of online courses or certifications that can enhance your skills and knowledge.

It is also important to seek feedback from your colleagues and superiors. Ask for constructive criticism and use it as an opportunity for growth. By continuously learning and developing, you can enhance your job satisfaction and advance in your career.

Embracing New Challenges and Responsibilities

Embracing new challenges and responsibilities is crucial for job satisfaction. When individuals step out of their comfort zones and take on new tasks, they are more likely to feel a sense of accomplishment and fulfillment.

To embrace new challenges and responsibilities, be open to learning new skills and taking on additional responsibilities. Volunteer for projects or assignments that align with your interests and goals. Seek opportunities to expand your knowledge and expertise in your field.

It is also important to have a growth mindset and view challenges as opportunities for learning and growth. Embrace failures as learning experiences and use them to improve and develop.

Finding Meaning and Purpose in Your Work

Finding meaning and purpose in your work is essential for job satisfaction. When individuals feel that their work has a positive impact and aligns with their values, they are more likely to feel fulfilled and motivated.

To find meaning and purpose in your work, reflect on the impact that your work has on others. Consider how your skills and expertise contribute to the success of your organization or the well-being of others. Connect with the mission and values of your organization and find ways to align your work with them.

It is also important to set meaningful goals for yourself. Identify what you want to achieve in your career and how it can contribute to your personal growth and the greater good. By finding meaning and purpose in your work, you can enhance your job satisfaction and overall well-being.

Celebrating Your Achievements and Successes

Celebrating achievements and successes is crucial for job satisfaction. When individuals acknowledge their accomplishments, they are more likely to feel valued and motivated in their jobs.

To celebrate achievements and successes, take time to reflect on your accomplishments. Acknowledge the progress you have made and the goals you have achieved. Share your successes with others and express gratitude for their support.

It is also important to reward yourself for your hard work. Treat yourself to something special or engage in activities that bring you joy. By celebrating your achievements, you can enhance your job satisfaction and maintain a positive mindset.

Knowing When it's Time to Move On

Knowing when it's time to move on from a job is crucial for job satisfaction. Sometimes, despite our best efforts, we may find ourselves in a situation where our needs are not being met or where we no longer feel fulfilled.

Signs that it's time to move on include feeling consistently unhappy or unfulfilled in your job, experiencing high levels of stress or burnout, and having limited opportunities for growth and development. It is important to listen to your intuition and trust your instincts.

If you decide that it's time to make a career change, take the time to explore your options and identify what you want in your next job. Update your resume and reach out to your network for support and guidance. Consider seeking the help of a career coach or counselor who can provide insights and assistance in the job search process.

In conclusion, job satisfaction is a crucial aspect of our professional lives. It has a significant impact on our overall well-being, productivity, and engagement in our jobs. By understanding the importance of job satisfaction and taking steps to enhance it, we can create fulfilling and meaningful careers. Remember to set clear career goals, assess your current job satisfaction level, analyze the factors affecting your job satisfaction, build positive relationships at work, create a healthy work-life balance, seek professional development opportunities, embrace new challenges and responsibilities, find meaning and purpose in your work, celebrate achievements and successes, and know when it's time to move on. By prioritizing job satisfaction, you can create a fulfilling and rewarding career.

Chapter 9: How to Boost Your Job Satisfaction

Job satisfaction is a crucial aspect of our professional lives. It refers to the level of contentment and fulfillment that individuals experience in their jobs. When employees are satisfied with their work, they are more likely to be engaged, motivated, and productive. Job satisfaction also has a significant impact on overall well-being and mental health. In this article, we will explore the importance of job satisfaction and provide tips on how to enhance it.

Understanding the Importance of Job Satisfaction

Job satisfaction is defined as the positive emotional state resulting from an individual's appraisal of their job or job experiences. It encompasses various factors such as the nature of work, relationships with colleagues and superiors, compensation, and opportunities for growth and development.

When employees are satisfied with their jobs, they are more likely to be committed to their organizations and have higher levels of productivity. They are also more likely to experience lower levels of stress and burnout. Job satisfaction has been linked to increased job performance, reduced turnover rates, and improved overall well-being.

On the other hand, job dissatisfaction can have detrimental effects on both individuals and organizations. Employees who are dissatisfied with their jobs may experience decreased motivation, lower productivity, and higher rates of absenteeism. They may also be more prone to physical and mental health issues such as anxiety and depression.

Identifying Your Career Goals

Setting clear career goals is essential for job satisfaction. When individuals have a sense of direction and purpose in their careers, they are more likely to feel fulfilled and motivated in their work.

To identify your career goals, start by reflecting on your interests, values, and skills. Consider what you enjoy doing and what you are passionate about. Think about your long-term aspirations and where you see yourself in the future. It can also be helpful to seek guidance from mentors or career counselors who can provide insights and support in the goal-setting process.

Assessing Your Current Job Satisfaction Level

Assessing your current job satisfaction level is crucial for understanding what aspects of your job are contributing to your satisfaction or dissatisfaction. By identifying areas of improvement, you can take steps to enhance your job satisfaction.

There are various methods for assessing job satisfaction. One common approach is to use surveys or questionnaires that measure different dimensions of job satisfaction, such as work-life balance, compensation, and opportunities for growth. Another method is to engage in self-reflection and journaling to explore your feelings and thoughts about your job.

Analyzing the Factors Affecting Your Job Satisfaction

Several factors can influence job satisfaction. By analyzing these factors, you can gain insights into what aspects of your job are contributing to your satisfaction or dissatisfaction.

Common factors affecting job satisfaction include the nature of work, relationships with colleagues and superiors, compensation and benefits, work-life balance, and opportunities for growth and development. It is essential to assess each of these factors and determine which ones are most important to you.

To analyze the factors affecting your job satisfaction, consider keeping a journal where you can reflect on your experiences at work. Take note of the tasks that bring you joy and fulfillment, as well as the ones that drain your energy. Pay attention to the relationships you have with your colleagues and superiors and how they impact your overall satisfaction.

Building Positive Relationships with Colleagues and Superiors

Positive relationships at work play a significant role in job satisfaction. When individuals have supportive and collaborative relationships with their colleagues and superiors, they are more likely to feel valued and motivated in their jobs.

To build positive relationships at work, start by being respectful and considerate towards your colleagues and superiors. Show appreciation for their contributions and offer support when needed. Foster open communication by actively listening to others and expressing your thoughts and ideas clearly.

It is also important to be a team player and collaborate effectively with others. By working together towards common goals, you can create a positive and supportive work environment.

Creating a Healthy Work-Life Balance

Achieving a healthy work-life balance is crucial for job satisfaction. When individuals have time for their personal lives and hobbies, they are more likely to feel fulfilled and satisfied in their jobs.

To create a healthy work-life balance, set boundaries between your work and personal life. Establish specific times for work and leisure activities and stick to them as much as possible. Prioritize self-care by engaging in activities that help you relax and recharge.

It is also important to communicate your needs and expectations with your colleagues and superiors. Let them know when you need time off or when you are feeling overwhelmed. By advocating for yourself, you can create a work environment that supports your well-being.

Seeking Professional Development Opportunities

Professional development is essential for job satisfaction. When individuals have opportunities to learn and grow in their careers, they are more likely to feel engaged and motivated in their work.

To seek professional development opportunities, start by identifying your areas of interest and areas for improvement. Consider attending workshops, conferences, or seminars related to your field.

Take advantage of online courses or certifications that can enhance your skills and knowledge.

It is also important to seek feedback from your colleagues and superiors. Ask for constructive criticism and use it as an opportunity for growth. By continuously learning and developing, you can enhance your job satisfaction and advance in your career.

Embracing New Challenges and Responsibilities

Embracing new challenges and responsibilities is crucial for job satisfaction. When individuals step out of their comfort zones and take on new tasks, they are more likely to feel a sense of accomplishment and fulfillment.

To embrace new challenges and responsibilities, be open to learning new skills and taking on additional responsibilities. Volunteer for projects or assignments that align with your interests and goals. Seek opportunities to expand your knowledge and expertise in your field.

It is also important to have a growth mindset and view challenges as opportunities for learning and growth. Embrace failures as learning experiences and use them to improve and develop.

Finding Meaning and Purpose in Your Work

Finding meaning and purpose in your work is essential for job satisfaction. When individuals feel that their work has a positive impact and aligns with their values, they are more likely to feel fulfilled and motivated.

To find meaning and purpose in your work, reflect on the impact that your work has on others. Consider how your skills and expertise contribute to the success of your organization or the well-being of others. Connect with the mission and values of your organization and find ways to align your work with them.

It is also important to set meaningful goals for yourself. Identify what you want to achieve in your career and how it can contribute to your personal growth and the greater good. By finding meaning and purpose in your work, you can enhance your job satisfaction and overall well-being.

Celebrating Your Achievements and Successes

Celebrating achievements and successes is crucial for job satisfaction. When individuals acknowledge their accomplishments, they are more likely to feel valued and motivated in their jobs.

To celebrate achievements and successes, take time to reflect on your accomplishments. Acknowledge the progress you have made and the goals you have achieved. Share your successes with others and express gratitude for their support.

It is also important to reward yourself for your hard work. Treat yourself to something special or engage in activities that bring you joy. By celebrating your achievements, you can enhance your job satisfaction and maintain a positive mindset.

Knowing When it's Time to Move On

Knowing when it's time to move on from a job is crucial for job satisfaction. Sometimes, despite our best efforts, we may find ourselves in a situation where our needs are not being met or where we no longer feel fulfilled.

Signs that it's time to move on include feeling consistently unhappy or unfulfilled in your job, experiencing high levels of stress or burnout, and having limited opportunities for growth and development. It is important to listen to your intuition and trust your instincts.

If you decide that it's time to make a career change, take the time to explore your options and identify what you want in your next job. Update your resume and reach out to your network for support and guidance. Consider seeking the help of a career coach or counselor who can provide insights and assistance in the job search process.

In conclusion, job satisfaction is a crucial aspect of our professional lives. It has a significant impact on our overall well-being, productivity, and engagement in our jobs. By understanding the importance of job satisfaction and taking steps to enhance it, we can create fulfilling and meaningful careers. Remember to set clear career goals, assess your current job satisfaction level, analyze the factors affecting your job satisfaction, build positive relationships at work, create a healthy work-life balance, seek professional development opportunities, embrace new challenges and responsibilities, find meaning and purpose in your work, celebrate achievements and successes, and know when it's time to move on. By prioritizing job satisfaction, you can create a fulfilling and rewarding career.

Chapter 10: Invisible Challenges

Hidden disabilities are conditions that are not immediately apparent to others. Unlike visible disabilities, which can be easily identified by physical characteristics or assistive devices, hidden disabilities are not readily noticeable. These disabilities can include physical, cognitive, and mental health conditions that impact a person's daily functioning and quality of life. Raising awareness about hidden disabilities is crucial in order to promote understanding, empathy, and support for individuals living with these conditions.

Common types of hidden disabilities

Hidden disabilities encompass a wide range of conditions. Physical hidden disabilities can include chronic pain, autoimmune disorders, and neurological conditions such as multiple sclerosis or fibromyalgia. Cognitive hidden disabilities may include learning disabilities, attention deficit hyperactivity disorder (ADHD), or autism spectrum disorder. Mental health conditions such as depression, anxiety disorders, or post-traumatic stress disorder (PTSD) can also be considered hidden disabilities.

Statistics on the prevalence of hidden disabilities vary depending on the specific condition being studied. However, it is estimated that approximately 10% of the global population lives with a hidden disability. These conditions can affect people of all ages and backgrounds, and the impact on daily life can vary greatly depending on the severity of the disability.

The challenges of living with a hidden disability

Living with a hidden disability presents unique challenges that are often not understood or recognized by others. One of the main difficulties is obtaining a proper diagnosis. Many hidden disabilities are complex and require specialized medical professionals to accurately identify and treat them. This process can be time-consuming, frustrating, and expensive.

Another challenge is the lack of understanding and support from others. Because hidden disabilities are not immediately apparent, individuals may face skepticism or disbelief when they try to explain their condition to others. This lack of validation can lead to feelings of isolation and frustration.

Feeling misunderstood is a common experience for those with hidden disabilities. Others may not fully grasp the impact that these conditions have on daily life, leading to misconceptions or dismissive attitudes. This can further contribute to feelings of isolation and can make it difficult for individuals to seek the support they need.

The emotional toll of hiding a disability

Hiding a disability can take a significant emotional toll on individuals. Fear of discrimination and stigma is a common concern. Many people with hidden disabilities worry that disclosing their condition will lead to negative consequences such as job loss, rejection, or social isolation. This fear can lead to a constant state of anxiety and stress.

Shame and guilt are also common emotions experienced by individuals with hidden disabilities. They may feel ashamed of their limitations or guilty for needing accommodations or support. These feelings can be internalized and contribute to low self-esteem and self-worth.

The impact on mental health is another significant aspect of hiding a disability. The constant need to conceal one's condition can lead to increased stress, anxiety, and depression. The pressure to appear "normal" or "able-bodied" can be overwhelming and can exacerbate existing mental health conditions.

The impact of stigma and stereotypes

Stigma and stereotypes surrounding disability can have a profound impact on individuals with hidden disabilities. Negative attitudes towards disability can perpetuate misconceptions and discrimination. Society often holds ableist beliefs that equate disability with weakness or incompetence, which can lead to exclusion and marginalization.

Stereotypes about what disability looks like can also be harmful. Many people associate disability with visible physical impairments, such as using a wheelchair or having a visible physical deformity. This narrow understanding of disability fails to recognize the diverse range of conditions that fall under the umbrella of hidden disabilities.

Stigma and stereotypes also affect access to resources and opportunities for individuals with hidden disabilities. Discrimination in employment, education, healthcare, and social settings can limit their ability to fully participate in society. This lack of access further perpetuates the cycle of marginalization and exclusion.

Navigating the workplace with a hidden disability

Navigating the workplace with a hidden disability can be particularly challenging. Individuals must decide whether to disclose their condition or keep it private. Disclosure can be beneficial in terms of accessing accommodations and support, but it also carries the risk of discrimination or harassment.

Requesting accommodations is an important step for individuals with hidden disabilities. Accommodations can include flexible work hours, modified job tasks, or assistive technology. However, individuals may face resistance or skepticism from employers who do not understand the impact of their condition.

Discrimination and harassment in the workplace are unfortunately common experiences for individuals with hidden disabilities. They may face negative attitudes, exclusion, or even termination based on their condition. It is important for individuals to know their rights and seek legal recourse if they experience discrimination.

Accessing accommodations and support

Legal protections exist to ensure that individuals with disabilities have equal access to opportunities and resources. In many countries, laws such as the Americans with Disabilities Act (ADA) in the United States or the Equality Act in the United Kingdom prohibit discrimination based on disability. These laws require employers, educational institutions, and public spaces to provide reasonable accommodations for individuals with disabilities.

Finding accommodations and support can be a daunting task for individuals with hidden disabilities. It is important to research available resources and organizations that specialize in supporting individuals with specific conditions. These organizations can provide guidance, advocacy, and connections to other individuals facing similar challenges.

Self-advocacy is also crucial in accessing accommodations and support. Individuals must learn to effectively communicate their needs and rights to others. This may involve educating employers, educators, or healthcare professionals about their condition and the impact it has on their daily life.

Strategies for self-advocacy

Self-advocacy is a skill that individuals with hidden disabilities must develop in order to navigate various aspects of life. Knowing one's rights is the first step in self-advocacy. Understanding the laws and regulations that protect individuals with disabilities can empower individuals to assert their rights and demand equal treatment.

Effective communication is another important aspect of self-advocacy. Individuals must learn to clearly and assertively communicate their needs, limitations, and accommodations to others. This may involve practicing self-advocacy skills such as assertiveness training or role-playing scenarios.

Building a support network is also crucial for self-advocacy. Connecting with others who have hidden disabilities can provide validation, guidance, and a sense of belonging. Peer support groups, online communities, or advocacy organizations can be valuable resources for individuals seeking support and empowerment.

Finding community and support

Finding community and support is essential for individuals with hidden disabilities. Connecting with others who share similar experiences can provide a sense of validation and understanding. Peer support groups or online communities can be valuable sources of information, advice, and empathy.

Joining advocacy groups and organizations is another way to find community and support. These groups often provide resources, educational materials, and opportunities for advocacy and activism. They can also serve as a platform for individuals to share their stories and raise awareness about hidden disabilities.

Peer support is particularly important for individuals with hidden disabilities. Having someone who understands the unique challenges they face can provide a sense of belonging and validation. Peer support can also offer practical advice and strategies for navigating various aspects of life with a hidden disability.

The importance of mental health and self-care

Managing mental health is crucial for individuals with hidden disabilities. The constant stress of hiding one's condition, fear of discrimination, and the challenges of daily life can take a toll on mental well-being. It is important for individuals to prioritize their mental health and seek appropriate support when needed.

Managing stress and anxiety is an important aspect of self-care for individuals with hidden disabilities. This may involve practicing relaxation techniques such as deep breathing, meditation, or mindfulness. Engaging in activities that bring joy and relaxation can also help reduce stress levels.

Seeking therapy and counseling can be beneficial for individuals with hidden disabilities. Therapy can provide a safe space to explore and process the emotions associated with living with a hidden disability. It can also offer practical strategies for coping with challenges and improving overall well-being.

Practicing self-care and self-compassion is essential for individuals with hidden disabilities. This may involve setting boundaries, prioritizing rest and relaxation, and engaging in activities that promote physical and emotional well-being. Taking care of oneself is not selfish, but rather a necessary part of managing a hidden disability.

Celebrating the strengths and resilience of those with hidden disabilities

It is important to recognize and celebrate the strengths and resilience of individuals with hidden disabilities. These individuals often face unique challenges on a daily basis, yet they continue to persevere and thrive. Highlighting their unique skills, abilities, and accomplishments can challenge stereotypes and promote a more inclusive and accepting society.

Recognizing the challenges that individuals with hidden disabilities overcome can foster empathy and understanding. It is important to acknowledge the strength it takes to navigate a world that often fails to recognize or accommodate their needs. By celebrating their resilience, we can create a more inclusive society that values diversity and promotes equal opportunities for all.

Promoting a more inclusive and accepting society requires collective action. It is important for individuals, communities, and institutions to actively work towards dismantling barriers and creating environments that are accessible to all. This includes challenging ableist attitudes, advocating for policy changes, and promoting inclusivity in all aspects of life.

Raising awareness about hidden disabilities is crucial in order to promote understanding, empathy, and support for individuals living with these conditions. Hidden disabilities encompass a wide range of physical, cognitive, and mental health conditions that impact daily functioning. Individuals with hidden disabilities face unique challenges, including difficulty obtaining a diagnosis, lack of understanding and support from others, and the emotional toll of hiding their condition.

Stigma and stereotypes surrounding disability can further exacerbate the challenges faced by individuals with hidden disabilities. Discrimination and exclusion can limit access to resources and opportunities. Navigating the workplace with a hidden disability can be particularly challenging, requiring individuals to make decisions about disclosure and accommodations.

Accessing accommodations and support is crucial for individuals with hidden disabilities. Legal protections exist to ensure equal access to opportunities and resources. Self-advocacy is an important skill that individuals must develop in order to navigate various aspects of life. Finding community and support is also essential for individuals with hidden disabilities, as it provides validation, guidance, and a sense of belonging.

Managing mental health and practicing self-care are important aspects of living with a hidden disability. It is crucial to recognize and celebrate the strengths and resilience of individuals with hidden disabilities. By promoting a more inclusive and accepting society, we can create a world that values diversity and supports the needs of all individuals.

Chapter 11: The Future is Equal: How We Can Create a More Inclusive Society

Equality is a fundamental principle that underpins a just and fair society. It is the belief that all individuals should have equal opportunities, rights, and treatment, regardless of their race, gender, socioeconomic status, or any other characteristic. Equality is not only a moral imperative but also a necessary condition for social progress and stability.

In an equal society, every individual has the chance to reach their full potential and contribute to the betterment of society. It ensures that no one is left behind or marginalized due to circumstances beyond their control. Equality promotes social cohesion, reduces social tensions, and fosters a sense of belonging and unity among diverse groups of people.

Understanding the Current State of Inequality

Despite the importance of equality, the current state of society is marked by significant disparities and inequalities. Income inequality is one of the most glaring examples of this. The gap between the rich and the poor has been widening in many countries, leading to social unrest and economic instability. This inequality in income distribution not only affects individuals' quality of life but also perpetuates cycles of poverty and disadvantage.

Education is another area where inequality persists. Access to quality education is often determined by socioeconomic status, with children from low-income families facing significant barriers to educational opportunities. This perpetuates a cycle of disadvantage, as individuals with limited access to education are less likely to secure well-paying jobs and escape poverty.

Healthcare is yet another area where inequality is prevalent. Access to quality healthcare services varies greatly depending on an individual's socioeconomic status, geographic location, and other factors. This leads to disparities in health outcomes, with marginalized communities often experiencing higher rates of illness and shorter life expectancies.

The Role of Education in Promoting Equality

Education plays a crucial role in promoting equality by providing individuals with the knowledge, skills, and opportunities they need to succeed in life. It empowers individuals to break free from the constraints of their circumstances and pursue their dreams.

Equal access to education is essential for creating a level playing field for all individuals. It ensures that every child, regardless of their background, has the opportunity to receive a quality education and reach their full potential. This requires addressing barriers such as poverty, discrimination, and lack of resources that prevent marginalized groups from accessing education.

Moreover, education can also challenge and change societal norms and attitudes that perpetuate inequality. By promoting values such as tolerance, respect, and empathy, education can help create a more inclusive and equitable society.

The Importance of Workplace Diversity and Inclusion

Workplace diversity and inclusion are crucial for promoting equality in society. A diverse workforce brings together individuals from different backgrounds, experiences, and perspectives, which leads to better decision-making, innovation, and problem-solving.

Diversity in the workplace also helps to break down stereotypes and biases by challenging preconceived notions about certain groups of people. It promotes understanding and empathy among colleagues and fosters a culture of respect and inclusion.

In addition to the social benefits, there are also economic advantages to having a diverse workforce. Studies have shown that companies with diverse teams are more likely to outperform their competitors and achieve higher financial returns. This is because diverse teams bring a wider range of ideas, creativity, and perspectives to the table, leading to better business outcomes.

The Impact of Technology on Equality

Technology has the potential to be a great equalizer in society by providing equal access to information, resources, and opportunities. However, the digital divide remains a significant barrier to achieving equality in the digital age.

Access to technology is not evenly distributed, with marginalized communities often lacking access to reliable internet connections, computers, and other digital devices. This limits their ability to participate fully in the digital economy and access educational resources, job opportunities, and essential services.

To bridge this digital divide, it is crucial to ensure equal access to technology for all individuals. This requires investment in infrastructure, digital literacy programs, and policies that promote affordable and accessible internet services.

The Need for Intersectionality in Fighting for Equality

Intersectionality is a concept that recognizes the interconnected nature of different forms of discrimination and oppression. It acknowledges that individuals can experience multiple forms of discrimination based on their race, gender, sexuality, disability, and other intersecting identities.

Addressing inequality requires an intersectional approach that takes into account the unique experiences and challenges faced by different groups of people. It recognizes that the fight for equality cannot be separated into separate silos but must address the complex ways in which different forms of discrimination intersect and compound each other.

For example, women of color may face unique challenges and barriers that are not experienced by white women or men of color. By understanding and addressing these intersectional experiences, we can develop more effective strategies for promoting equality and social justice.

Addressing Systemic Discrimination and Bias

Systemic discrimination refers to the ways in which institutions, policies, and practices perpetuate inequality and disadvantage certain groups of people. It is often embedded in societal structures and norms, making it difficult to identify and address.

Implicit biases are another form of discrimination that can perpetuate inequality. These biases are unconscious attitudes or stereotypes that affect our understanding, actions, and decisions without our conscious awareness. They can lead to discriminatory practices in areas such as hiring, promotion, and access to resources.

Addressing systemic discrimination and implicit biases requires a multi-faceted approach. It involves raising awareness about these issues, implementing policies and practices that promote equality, and holding institutions accountable for their actions.

Strategies for Achieving Gender Equality

Gender equality is a critical aspect of overall equality in society. Despite progress in recent decades, gender disparities persist in many areas, including pay, representation in leadership positions, and access to education and healthcare.

To achieve gender equality, it is essential to address the root causes of these disparities. This includes promoting equal pay for equal work, implementing policies that support work-life balance, and challenging gender stereotypes and biases.

Increasing the representation of women in leadership positions is also crucial for achieving gender equality. This requires creating a supportive and inclusive work environment that allows women to thrive and advance in their careers.

Creating Inclusive Communities and Public Spaces

Creating inclusive communities and public spaces is essential for promoting equality and ensuring that everyone feels welcome and valued. This includes designing public spaces that are accessible to individuals with disabilities, providing affordable housing options for low-income families, and promoting cultural diversity and inclusion.

Inclusive communities also foster social cohesion and a sense of belonging among diverse groups of people. They provide opportunities for individuals to connect, collaborate, and learn from one another, leading to a more harmonious and equitable society.

The Role of Government in Promoting Equality

The government plays a crucial role in promoting equality by enacting policies and laws that protect individuals' rights and ensure equal opportunities and treatment for all. This includes implementing anti-discrimination laws, promoting affirmative action programs, and investing in social welfare programs that support marginalized communities.

Government policies can also help address systemic discrimination by promoting diversity and inclusion in public institutions, such as schools, hospitals, and government agencies. This requires proactive measures to ensure equal representation and participation of diverse groups in decision-making processes.

Working Together to Create a More Equal Future

Achieving equality in society is a complex and ongoing process that requires the collective efforts of individuals, organizations, and governments. It requires addressing the root causes of inequality, challenging discriminatory practices and attitudes, and creating inclusive systems and structures.

By recognizing the importance of equality and taking action to promote it, we can create a more just, fair, and prosperous society for all. It is up to each one of us to play our part in working towards a more equal future.

Chapter 12: The Future is Equal

Equality is a fundamental principle that underpins a just and fair society. It is the belief that all individuals should have equal opportunities, rights, and treatment, regardless of their race, gender, socioeconomic status, or any other characteristic. Equality is not only a moral imperative but also a necessary condition for social progress and stability.

In an equal society, every individual has the chance to reach their full potential and contribute to the betterment of society. It ensures that no one is left behind or marginalized due to circumstances beyond their control. Equality promotes social cohesion, reduces social tensions, and fosters a sense of belonging and unity among diverse groups of people.

Understanding the Current State of Inequality

Despite the importance of equality, the current state of society is marked by significant disparities and inequalities. Income inequality is one of the most glaring examples of this. The gap between the rich and the poor has been widening in many countries, leading to social unrest and economic instability. This inequality in income distribution not only affects individuals' quality of life but also perpetuates cycles of poverty and disadvantage.

Education is another area where inequality persists. Access to quality education is often determined by socioeconomic status, with children from low-income families facing significant barriers to educational opportunities. This perpetuates a cycle of disadvantage, as individuals with limited access to education are less likely to secure well-paying jobs and escape poverty.

Healthcare is yet another area where inequality is prevalent. Access to quality healthcare services varies greatly depending on an individual's socioeconomic status, geographic location, and other factors. This leads to disparities in health outcomes, with marginalized communities often experiencing higher rates of illness and shorter life expectancies.

The Role of Education in Promoting Equality

Education plays a crucial role in promoting equality by providing individuals with the knowledge, skills, and opportunities they need to succeed in life. It empowers individuals to break free from the constraints of their circumstances and pursue their dreams.

Equal access to education is essential for creating a level playing field for all individuals. It ensures that every child, regardless of their background, has the opportunity to receive a quality education and reach their full potential. This requires addressing barriers such as poverty, discrimination, and lack of resources that prevent marginalized groups from accessing education.

Moreover, education can also challenge and change societal norms and attitudes that perpetuate inequality. By promoting values such as tolerance, respect, and empathy, education can help create a more inclusive and equitable society.

The Importance of Workplace Diversity and Inclusion

Workplace diversity and inclusion are crucial for promoting equality in society. A diverse workforce brings together individuals from different backgrounds, experiences, and perspectives, which leads to better decision-making, innovation, and problem-solving.

Diversity in the workplace also helps to break down stereotypes and biases by challenging preconceived notions about certain groups of people. It promotes understanding and empathy among colleagues and fosters a culture of respect and inclusion.

In addition to the social benefits, there are also economic advantages to having a diverse workforce. Studies have shown that companies with diverse teams are more likely to outperform their competitors and achieve higher financial returns. This is because diverse teams bring a wider range of ideas, creativity, and perspectives to the table, leading to better business outcomes.

The Impact of Technology on Equality

Technology has the potential to be a great equalizer in society by providing equal access to information, resources, and opportunities. However, the digital divide remains a significant barrier to achieving equality in the digital age.

Access to technology is not evenly distributed, with marginalized communities often lacking access to reliable internet connections, computers, and other digital devices. This limits their ability to participate fully in the digital economy and access educational resources, job opportunities, and essential services.

To bridge this digital divide, it is crucial to ensure equal access to technology for all individuals. This requires investment in infrastructure, digital literacy programs, and policies that promote affordable and accessible internet services.

The Need for Intersectionality in Fighting for Equality

Intersectionality is a concept that recognizes the interconnected nature of different forms of discrimination and oppression. It acknowledges that individuals can experience multiple forms of discrimination based on their race, gender, sexuality, disability, and other intersecting identities.

Addressing inequality requires an intersectional approach that takes into account the unique experiences and challenges faced by different groups of people. It recognizes that the fight for equality cannot be separated into separate silos but must address the complex ways in which different forms of discrimination intersect and compound each other.

For example, women of color may face unique challenges and barriers that are not experienced by white women or men of color. By understanding and addressing these intersectional experiences, we can develop more effective strategies for promoting equality and social justice.

Addressing Systemic Discrimination and Bias

Systemic discrimination refers to the ways in which institutions, policies, and practices perpetuate inequality and disadvantage certain groups of people. It is often embedded in societal structures and norms, making it difficult to identify and address.

Implicit biases are another form of discrimination that can perpetuate inequality. These biases are unconscious attitudes or stereotypes that affect our understanding, actions, and decisions without our conscious awareness. They can lead to discriminatory practices in areas such as hiring, promotion, and access to resources.

Addressing systemic discrimination and implicit biases requires a multi-faceted approach. It involves raising awareness about these issues, implementing policies and practices that promote equality, and holding institutions accountable for their actions.

Strategies for Achieving Gender Equality

Gender equality is a critical aspect of overall equality in society. Despite progress in recent decades, gender disparities persist in many areas, including pay, representation in leadership positions, and access to education and healthcare.

To achieve gender equality, it is essential to address the root causes of these disparities. This includes promoting equal pay for equal work, implementing policies that support work-life balance, and challenging gender stereotypes and biases.

Increasing the representation of women in leadership positions is also crucial for achieving gender equality. This requires creating a supportive and inclusive work environment that allows women to thrive and advance in their careers.

Creating Inclusive Communities and Public Spaces

Creating inclusive communities and public spaces is essential for promoting equality and ensuring that everyone feels welcome and valued. This includes designing public spaces that are accessible to individuals with disabilities, providing affordable housing options for low-income families, and promoting cultural diversity and inclusion.

Inclusive communities also foster social cohesion and a sense of belonging among diverse groups of people. They provide opportunities for individuals to connect, collaborate, and learn from one another, leading to a more harmonious and equitable society.

The Role of Government in Promoting Equality

The government plays a crucial role in promoting equality by enacting policies and laws that protect individuals' rights and ensure equal opportunities and treatment for all. This includes implementing anti-discrimination laws, promoting affirmative action programs, and investing in social welfare programs that support marginalized communities.

Government policies can also help address systemic discrimination by promoting diversity and inclusion in public institutions, such as schools, hospitals, and government agencies. This requires proactive measures to ensure equal representation and participation of diverse groups in decision-making processes.

Working Together to Create a More Equal Future

Achieving equality in society is a complex and ongoing process that requires the collective efforts of individuals, organizations, and governments. It requires addressing the root causes of inequality, challenging discriminatory practices and attitudes, and creating inclusive systems and structures.

By recognizing the importance of equality and taking action to promote it, we can create a more just, fair, and prosperous society for all. It is up to each one of us to play our part in working towards a more equal future.

Chapter 13: Task Modification 101: A Beginner's Guide to Customizing Your Workload

Task modification refers to the process of making changes to tasks in order to improve productivity and reduce stress. It involves assessing your workload, identifying tasks that can be modified, and implementing changes to streamline, improve, or personalize those tasks. Task modification is important because it allows individuals to work more efficiently, effectively, and in a way that aligns with their preferences and strengths.

By modifying tasks, individuals can optimize their work processes and achieve better results. This can lead to increased productivity, as tasks are completed more quickly and with less effort. Additionally, task modification can help reduce stress by eliminating unnecessary or repetitive tasks, allowing individuals to focus on the most important and meaningful aspects of their work.

Understanding Your Workload: Identifying Tasks that Can be Modified

To effectively modify tasks, it is important to first assess your workload and identify tasks that can be modified. This involves taking a step back and evaluating the tasks you currently perform on a regular basis. Look for tasks that are time-consuming, repetitive, or do not contribute significantly to your overall goals or objectives.

For example, administrative tasks such as data entry or filing paperwork are often prime candidates for modification. These tasks can often be automated or delegated to free up time for more important and strategic work. Similarly, tasks that require excessive coordination or communication can often be streamlined by implementing better systems or tools.

Prioritizing Tasks: How to Decide Which Tasks to Modify

Before modifying tasks, it is important to prioritize them based on their importance and urgency. This will help ensure that you are focusing on the most critical tasks first and making the necessary modifications to improve their efficiency or effectiveness.

When prioritizing tasks, consider factors such as deadlines, impact on overall goals, and dependencies on other tasks or team members. By focusing on high-priority tasks first, you can maximize the impact of your modifications and achieve the greatest results.

Modifying Tasks for Efficiency: Streamlining Your Workload

One of the key objectives of task modification is to streamline tasks in order to save time and effort. There are several techniques that can be used to achieve this, such as automation, delegation, and process improvement.

Automation involves using technology or tools to automate repetitive or time-consuming tasks. For example, using software to automatically generate reports or scheduling tools to automate meeting invitations can save significant time and effort.

Delegation involves assigning tasks to others who are better suited or have more capacity to complete them. This can free up your time to focus on more important or strategic work. It is important to delegate tasks effectively by clearly communicating expectations and providing necessary support or resources.

Process improvement involves analyzing and optimizing the steps involved in completing a task. This can include eliminating unnecessary steps, simplifying processes, or implementing better tools or systems. By streamlining processes, tasks can be completed more efficiently and with less effort.

Modifying Tasks for Effectiveness: Enhancing the Quality of Your Work

In addition to improving efficiency, task modification can also be used to enhance the quality of your work. This involves making changes that improve the accuracy, thoroughness, or impact of tasks.

One technique for improving effectiveness is by implementing quality control measures. This can include double-checking work for errors or inconsistencies, seeking feedback from others, or conducting thorough reviews before finalizing tasks. By ensuring that tasks are completed accurately and thoroughly, the overall quality of work can be improved.

Another technique for enhancing effectiveness is by incorporating best practices or industry standards into tasks. This involves researching and implementing proven methods or approaches that have been shown to produce better results. By adopting these best practices, tasks can be completed in a way that maximizes their impact and effectiveness.

Modifying Tasks for Personalization: Tailoring Your Workload to Your Needs

Task modification can also be used to personalize tasks to fit your preferences and strengths. This involves customizing tasks in a way that allows you to work in a manner that is most comfortable or effective for you.

One technique for personalizing tasks is by adapting them to align with your preferred working style. For example, if you are a visual learner, you may find it helpful to create visual aids or diagrams to assist with understanding and completing tasks. Similarly, if you prefer working in short bursts of focused activity, you may find it beneficial to break tasks into smaller, manageable chunks.

Another technique for personalization is by leveraging your strengths and skills. Identify tasks that align with your strengths and find ways to incorporate them into your workload. This can help increase your motivation and engagement, as well as improve the quality of your work.

Tools and Techniques for Task Modification: Tips for Customizing Your Workload

There are several tools and techniques that can be used for task modification. These tools and techniques can help individuals customize their workload to fit their needs and preferences.

One tool that can be used is project management software. This type of software allows individuals to track and manage tasks, set deadlines, and collaborate with others. By using project management software, individuals can streamline their workload and ensure that tasks are completed on time and within budget.

Another tool that can be helpful is task management apps or tools. These tools allow individuals to create to-do lists, set reminders, and track progress on tasks. By using task management apps, individuals can stay organized and focused on their priorities.

In addition to tools, there are also several techniques that can be used for task modification. One technique is time blocking, which involves scheduling specific blocks of time for different tasks or activities. This helps individuals allocate their time effectively and ensures that important tasks are given the necessary attention.

Another technique is the Pomodoro Technique, which involves working in short bursts of focused activity followed by short breaks. This technique can help individuals maintain focus and productivity throughout the day.

Overcoming Challenges: Addressing Obstacles in Task Modification

While task modification can bring many benefits, there are also common challenges that individuals may face when implementing changes. It is important to be aware of these challenges and develop strategies for overcoming them.

One common challenge is resistance to change. People may be resistant to modifying tasks because they are comfortable with their current processes or fear that changes will disrupt their workflow. To overcome this challenge, it is important to communicate the benefits of task modification and involve others in the process. By involving others and addressing their concerns, resistance to change can be minimized.

Another challenge is lack of resources or support. Task modification may require additional resources or support, such as training or access to new tools or technology. To overcome this challenge, it is important to identify and communicate the necessary resources or support needed for task modification. This can involve seeking approval or budget allocation from supervisors or collaborating with others who can provide the necessary resources.

Communicating Changes: How to Inform Your Team or Supervisor of Modified Tasks

When modifying tasks, it is important to communicate these changes to others, such as your team or supervisor. Effective communication ensures that everyone is aware of the modifications and can adjust their expectations or workflows accordingly.

When communicating changes, it is important to be clear and concise. Clearly explain the reasons for the modifications and how they will impact others. Provide any necessary instructions or guidelines for implementing the changes and address any questions or concerns that may arise.

It can also be helpful to involve others in the decision-making process when modifying tasks. This can help build buy-in and ensure that everyone feels included and valued in the process. By involving others, you can also benefit from their insights and perspectives, which may lead to further improvements or refinements in the modifications.

Evaluating Results: Assessing the Impact of Task Modification on Your Workload

After implementing task modifications, it is important to evaluate the impact of these changes on your workload. This involves assessing whether the modifications have achieved the desired results and identifying any areas for further improvement.

There are several methods that can be used to evaluate results. One method is to track key performance indicators (KPIs) related to the modified tasks. For example, if the goal was to improve efficiency, you could track metrics such as time saved or tasks completed per hour. If the goal was to improve effectiveness, you could track metrics such as customer satisfaction or quality ratings.

Another method is to gather feedback from others, such as team members or supervisors. This can involve conducting surveys or interviews to gather their perspectives on the impact of the modifications. By gathering feedback, you can gain valuable insights and identify any areas for improvement or refinement.

The Benefits of Task Modification and How to Get Started

In conclusion, task modification is a powerful tool for improving productivity and reducing stress. By assessing your workload, identifying tasks that can be modified, and implementing changes to streamline, improve, or personalize those tasks, you can optimize your work processes and achieve better results.

The benefits of task modification are numerous. It allows individuals to work more efficiently, effectively, and in a way that aligns with their preferences and strengths. It can save time and effort by streamlining tasks, improve the quality of work by enhancing effectiveness, and increase motivation and engagement by personalizing tasks.

To get started with task modification, begin by assessing your workload and identifying tasks that can be modified. Prioritize these tasks based on their importance and urgency, and then implement changes to streamline, improve, or personalize them. Use tools and techniques such as project management software, task management apps, time blocking, or the Pomodoro Technique to help customize your workload.

Remember to communicate changes to others and evaluate the impact of task modifications on your workload. By continuously assessing and refining your modifications, you can ensure that you are achieving the desired results and maximizing the benefits of task modification.

Chapter 14: From Chaos to Calm: The Art of Emotional Regulation

Emotional regulation refers to the ability to manage and control one's emotions effectively. It involves recognizing and understanding one's emotions, as well as being able to respond to them in a healthy and adaptive manner. Emotional regulation is an essential skill that plays a crucial role in our daily lives. It helps us navigate through various situations, maintain mental well-being, and build healthy relationships.

The Importance of Emotional Regulation

Emotional regulation has a significant impact on mental health. When we are unable to regulate our emotions, we may experience heightened levels of stress, anxiety, and depression. Unregulated emotions can lead to impulsive behaviors, difficulty concentrating, and a decreased ability to cope with life's challenges. On the other hand, individuals who possess strong emotional regulation skills are better equipped to handle stress, maintain positive mental health, and experience overall well-being.

Furthermore, emotional regulation plays a vital role in our relationships. When we are unable to regulate our emotions, we may lash out at others or withdraw from social interactions. This can strain relationships and lead to misunderstandings and conflicts. On the contrary, individuals who can regulate their emotions effectively are more likely to communicate their needs and feelings in a healthy manner, leading to stronger and more fulfilling relationships.

"

The Link Between Emotions and Behavior

Emotions have a profound influence on our behavior. When we experience intense emotions such as anger or sadness, it can be challenging to think rationally and make sound decisions. Unregulated emotions can lead to impulsive actions that we may later regret. For example, someone who is overwhelmed with anger may engage in aggressive behavior or say hurtful things without considering the consequences.

Moreover, unregulated emotions can have long-term consequences on our well-being. Chronic stress resulting from unregulated emotions can lead to physical health problems such as high blood pressure, heart disease, and weakened immune system. It can also contribute to the development of mental health disorders such as anxiety and depression. Therefore, it is crucial to develop emotional regulation skills to prevent these negative outcomes.

The Science Behind Emotional Regulation

Emotional regulation is a complex process that involves various regions of the brain. The prefrontal cortex, which is responsible for executive functions such as decision-making and impulse control, plays a crucial role in emotional regulation. When we experience intense emotions, the prefrontal cortex helps us regulate our emotional responses by inhibiting impulsive reactions and allowing us to think rationally.

However, chronic stress can impair the functioning of the prefrontal cortex, making it more challenging to regulate emotions effectively. Stress activates the amygdala, which is responsible for processing emotions, and can override the prefrontal cortex's control.

This can lead to heightened emotional responses and difficulty in regulating emotions.

The Role of Mindfulness in Emotional Regulation

Mindfulness is a practice that involves paying attention to the present moment without judgment. It allows us to observe our thoughts, emotions, and bodily sensations without getting caught up in them. Mindfulness can be a powerful tool for emotional regulation as it helps us become aware of our emotions and respond to them in a non-reactive manner.

By practicing mindfulness, we can develop a greater sense of self-awareness and recognize when we are experiencing intense emotions. This awareness allows us to take a step back and choose how we want to respond rather than reacting impulsively. Mindfulness also helps us cultivate a sense of acceptance towards our emotions, allowing us to experience them without judgment or resistance.

Techniques for Regulating Emotions

There are various techniques that can help with emotional regulation. One important step is identifying triggers - situations or events that elicit intense emotional responses. By recognizing these triggers, we can anticipate and prepare for them, allowing us to respond in a more controlled manner.

Self-soothing techniques can also be helpful in regulating emotions. These techniques involve engaging in activities that promote relaxation and calmness, such as deep breathing, taking a warm bath, or listening to soothing music. Engaging in self-soothing activities can help reduce the intensity of emotions and provide a sense of comfort.

Distraction techniques can also be effective in regulating emotions. These techniques involve redirecting our attention away from the intense emotions and towards something more positive or neutral. For example, engaging in a hobby, going for a walk, or talking to a friend can help shift our focus and provide a temporary relief from intense emotions.

Breathing Exercises for Emotional Regulation

Breathing exercises are a simple yet powerful tool for emotional regulation. When we are stressed or experiencing intense emotions, our breathing tends to become shallow and rapid. This can further exacerbate our emotional state. By practicing deep breathing exercises, we can activate the body's relaxation response and promote a sense of calmness.

Deep breathing exercises involve taking slow, deep breaths in through the nose and exhaling slowly through the mouth. This type of breathing activates the parasympathetic nervous system, which is responsible for promoting relaxation and reducing stress. By practicing deep breathing regularly, we can train our body to respond to stressful situations with a calmer and more controlled demeanor.

There are various types of breathing exercises that can be used for emotional regulation. One example is diaphragmatic breathing, which involves breathing deeply into the diaphragm rather than shallowly into the chest. Another example is box breathing, which involves inhaling for a count of four, holding the breath for a count of four, exhaling for a count of four, and holding the breath out for a count of four. Experimenting with different types of breathing exercises can help find what works best for each individual.

Cognitive Behavioral Therapy and Emotional Regulation

Cognitive Behavioral Therapy (CBT) is a therapeutic approach that focuses on identifying and changing negative thought patterns and behaviors. It can be highly effective in helping individuals develop emotional regulation skills. CBT helps individuals recognize the connection between their thoughts, emotions, and behaviors and provides them with tools to challenge and change unhelpful patterns.

In CBT, individuals learn to identify and challenge negative thoughts that contribute to intense emotional responses. By replacing negative thoughts with more realistic and positive ones, individuals can regulate their emotions more effectively. CBT also helps individuals develop coping strategies and problem-solving skills, allowing them to respond to challenging situations in a more adaptive manner.

The Benefits of Emotional Regulation

Developing emotional regulation skills can have numerous benefits for mental health, relationships, and overall well-being. Improved mental health is one of the primary benefits of emotional regulation. By regulating our emotions effectively, we can reduce stress, anxiety, and depression, leading to improved mental well-being.

Emotional regulation also plays a crucial role in building and maintaining healthy relationships. When we can regulate our emotions, we are better able to communicate our needs and feelings in a healthy manner. This leads to stronger connections and more fulfilling relationships with others.

Furthermore, emotional regulation can increase productivity and performance in various areas of life. When we are able to regulate our emotions, we can think more clearly, make better decisions, and stay focused on our goals. This can lead to increased productivity at work or school and overall success in life.

Implementing Emotional Regulation in Daily Life

Implementing emotional regulation in daily life requires consistent effort and practice. One way to start is by creating a self-care routine that includes activities that promote relaxation and emotional well-being. This can include engaging in hobbies, practicing mindfulness or meditation, exercising regularly, or spending time with loved ones.

Practicing mindfulness is another essential aspect of implementing emotional regulation in daily life. By incorporating mindfulness into our daily routines, we can develop a greater sense of self-awareness and respond to our emotions in a more controlled manner. This can be done through formal mindfulness practices such as meditation or through informal practices such as mindful eating or mindful walking.

Seeking professional help is also an option for individuals who are struggling with emotional regulation. A therapist or counselor can provide guidance and support in developing emotional regulation skills. They can help individuals identify triggers, develop coping strategies, and work through any underlying issues that may be contributing to difficulties in emotional regulation.

The Journey to Emotional Calmness

Emotional regulation is a lifelong journey that requires continuous effort and practice. By understanding the importance of emotional regulation and implementing various techniques and strategies, individuals can achieve emotional calmness and improve their overall well-being. Developing emotional regulation skills can lead to improved mental health, better relationships, and increased productivity in various areas of life. So, let us embark on this journey towards emotional regulation and experience the benefits it brings.

Chapter 15: The Science of Productivity

In today's fast-paced world, productivity has become more important than ever. With the constant demands of work, personal life, and technology, it can be challenging to stay focused and accomplish tasks efficiently. However, being productive is crucial for both personal and professional success. It allows us to make the most of our time, achieve our goals, and maintain a healthy work-life balance.

Productivity is not just about getting things done quickly; it's about working smarter, not harder. When we are productive, we can accomplish more in less time, freeing up valuable hours for leisure activities or spending time with loved ones. Additionally, being productive can reduce stress levels and increase overall satisfaction with our work and personal lives.

The Brain's Default Mode Network: How it Affects Your Work Habits

The brain's default mode network (DMN) is a network of brain regions that are active when we are not engaged in any specific task. It is responsible for mind-wandering, daydreaming, and self-referential thinking. While the DMN is essential for creativity and introspection, it can also hinder productivity.

When the DMN is active during work tasks, it can lead to distractions and decreased focus. To improve productivity, it is important to activate the task-positive network (TPN), which is responsible for focused attention and goal-directed behavior.

There are several ways to activate the TPN and reduce the activity of the DMN. One effective method is mindfulness meditation. By practicing mindfulness, we can train our brains to stay present and focused on the task at hand. Other techniques include setting clear goals, breaking tasks into smaller manageable chunks, and eliminating distractions such as social media or email notifications.

The Role of Dopamine in Motivation and Productivity

Dopamine is a neurotransmitter that plays a crucial role in motivation and reward. It is often referred to as the "feel-good" chemical because it is released when we experience pleasure or achieve a goal. Dopamine is also involved in regulating attention, focus, and decision-making.

To boost productivity, it is important to increase dopamine levels in the brain. One way to do this is by setting achievable goals and rewarding yourself when you accomplish them. This can create a positive feedback loop that motivates you to continue working towards your objectives.

Another way to increase dopamine levels is through exercise. Physical activity has been shown to release dopamine in the brain, leading to improved mood and increased motivation. Additionally, engaging in activities that you enjoy and find fulfilling can also boost dopamine levels and enhance productivity.

The Science of Procrastination: Why We Delay and How to Overcome It

Procrastination is a common phenomenon that affects many people's productivity. It is the act of delaying or postponing tasks, often in favor of more pleasurable or easier activities. While procrastination may provide temporary relief, it can have negative consequences on our productivity and overall well-being.

The science behind procrastination lies in the brain's reward system. When we engage in pleasurable activities such as watching TV or scrolling through social media, our brain releases dopamine, which reinforces the behavior. This can make it difficult to resist immediate gratification and prioritize long-term goals.

To overcome procrastination, it is important to understand the underlying reasons for delaying tasks. This could be due to fear of failure, perfectionism, or feeling overwhelmed by the magnitude of the task. Once you identify the root cause of your procrastination, you can develop strategies to address it.

Some effective strategies for overcoming procrastination include breaking tasks into smaller, more manageable steps, setting deadlines for each step, and using tools such as timers or productivity apps to stay on track. It can also be helpful to create a supportive environment by eliminating distractions and seeking accountability from a friend or colleague.

The Power of Habits: How to Form Good Ones and Break Bad Ones

Habits play a significant role in our productivity. They are automatic behaviors that we perform without conscious thought, allowing us to conserve mental energy and focus on more complex tasks. However, not all habits are beneficial for productivity.

To improve productivity, it is important to form good habits and break bad ones. Good habits can include setting a consistent schedule, prioritizing tasks, and practicing self-discipline. Breaking bad habits may involve identifying triggers and finding alternative behaviors to replace them.

One effective strategy for forming good habits is the habit loop, which consists of three components: the cue, the routine, and the reward. By identifying the cue that triggers a habit, you can consciously choose a new routine that aligns with your productivity goals. Additionally, rewarding yourself after completing a habit can reinforce the behavior and make it more likely to stick.

Breaking bad habits can be more challenging, as they are often deeply ingrained in our routines. However, by replacing the routine with a healthier alternative and being mindful of the triggers that lead to the habit, it is possible to break free from unproductive behaviors.

The Impact of Multitasking on Productivity and Brain Functioning

Multitasking is often seen as a desirable skill in today's fast-paced world. However, research has shown that multitasking can actually decrease productivity and impair brain functioning.

When we multitask, our attention becomes divided between multiple tasks, leading to decreased focus and increased errors. Additionally, switching between tasks can result in a cognitive cost known as "switching time," where our brains need time to refocus on the new task.

To improve productivity, it is important to avoid multitasking and instead focus on one task at a time. This allows us to give our full attention to the task at hand and complete it more efficiently. It can also reduce stress levels and improve the quality of our work.

One effective strategy for avoiding multitasking is to prioritize tasks and allocate dedicated time blocks for each one. By creating a schedule and sticking to it, you can ensure that you have uninterrupted time to focus on important tasks. Additionally, eliminating distractions such as phone notifications or email alerts can help maintain focus and prevent multitasking.

The Benefits of Taking Breaks: How to Optimize Your Rest Time

Taking breaks is essential for maintaining productivity and preventing burnout. Research has shown that regular breaks can improve focus, creativity, and overall well-being.

When we work for extended periods without breaks, our attention and cognitive resources become depleted, leading to decreased productivity and increased errors. Taking short breaks throughout the day allows our brains to recharge and replenish these resources, leading to improved performance.

To optimize rest time, it is important to engage in activities that promote relaxation and rejuvenation. This could include going for a walk, practicing deep breathing exercises, or engaging in a hobby or leisure activity. Additionally, incorporating mindfulness practices during breaks can help reduce stress levels and improve focus.

It is also important to schedule regular longer breaks, such as lunch breaks or vacation time. These extended periods of rest allow us to fully disconnect from work and recharge both physically and mentally. By prioritizing rest and relaxation, we can maintain high levels of productivity and prevent burnout.

The Science of Sleep: How it Affects Your Productivity and Brain Health

Sleep plays a crucial role in our productivity and overall brain health. It is during sleep that our brains consolidate memories, process information, and restore energy levels.

Lack of sleep can have detrimental effects on productivity. It impairs cognitive function, attention, and decision-making abilities. Additionally, chronic sleep deprivation has been linked to an increased risk of mental health disorders such as depression and anxiety.

To improve productivity, it is important to prioritize sleep and establish a consistent sleep routine. This includes going to bed and waking up at the same time each day, creating a sleep-friendly environment, and practicing relaxation techniques before bed.

Additionally, practicing good sleep hygiene can help improve the quality of your sleep. This includes avoiding caffeine and stimulating activities before bed, limiting exposure to screens, and creating a relaxing bedtime routine.

The Importance of Mindfulness: How to Stay Focused and Calm

Mindfulness is the practice of being fully present and aware of the present moment. It has been shown to improve focus, reduce stress levels, and enhance overall well-being.

In today's fast-paced world, it can be challenging to stay focused and calm. Our minds are often filled with thoughts about the past or worries about the future. However, by practicing mindfulness, we can train our brains to stay present and focused on the task at hand.

There are several ways to incorporate mindfulness into your daily routine. This could include practicing meditation, engaging in mindful breathing exercises, or simply taking a few moments throughout the day to pause and observe your surroundings.

By cultivating a mindfulness practice, you can improve your ability to stay focused, reduce stress levels, and enhance your overall productivity.

The Role of Nutrition and Exercise in Boosting Productivity

Nutrition and exercise play a significant role in our productivity. A healthy diet and regular physical activity can provide us with the energy and mental clarity needed to perform at our best.

Eating a balanced diet that includes whole foods, fruits, vegetables, lean proteins, and healthy fats can provide us with the nutrients needed for optimal brain function. Additionally, staying hydrated throughout the day is essential for maintaining cognitive function and preventing fatigue.

Regular exercise has been shown to improve cognitive function, memory, and overall mood. It increases blood flow to the brain, stimulates the release of endorphins (feel-good hormones), and reduces stress levels. Incorporating physical activity into your daily routine, such as going for a walk or practicing yoga, can help boost productivity and enhance overall well-being.

Applying the Science of Productivity to Your Work Habits

In conclusion, productivity is crucial for personal and professional success in today's fast-paced world. By understanding the science behind productivity and implementing strategies to improve focus, motivation, and well-being, we can make the most of our time and achieve our goals.

Some key takeaways from this article include:

- Activating the task-positive network and reducing the activity of the default mode network to improve focus and productivity.

- Increasing dopamine levels through goal-setting, rewarding yourself, and engaging in activities you enjoy.

- Overcoming procrastination by understanding the underlying reasons for delaying tasks and implementing strategies such as breaking tasks into smaller steps and seeking accountability.

- Forming good habits and breaking bad ones through the habit loop and mindful awareness of triggers.

- Avoiding multitasking and focusing on one task at a time to improve productivity and reduce cognitive load.

- Taking regular breaks to recharge and optimize rest time.

- Prioritizing sleep and practicing good sleep hygiene to improve productivity and brain health.

- Cultivating mindfulness to stay focused, reduce stress levels, and enhance overall well-being.

- Nourishing your body with a balanced diet and engaging in regular physical activity to boost energy levels and cognitive function.

By applying these strategies to your work habits, you can prioritize productivity, achieve your goals, and lead a more fulfilling life. Remember that productivity is not about working harder; it's about working smarter and making the most of your time.

Chapter 15: The Science of Productivity

In today's fast-paced world, productivity has become more important than ever. With the constant demands of work, personal life, and technology, it can be challenging to stay focused and accomplish tasks efficiently. However, being productive is crucial for both personal and professional success. It allows us to make the most of our time, achieve our goals, and maintain a healthy work-life balance.

Productivity is not just about getting things done quickly; it's about working smarter, not harder. When we are productive, we can accomplish more in less time, freeing up valuable hours for leisure activities or spending time with loved ones. Additionally, being productive can reduce stress levels and increase overall satisfaction with our work and personal lives.

The Brain's Default Mode Network: How it Affects Your Work Habits

The brain's default mode network (DMN) is a network of brain regions that are active when we are not engaged in any specific task. It is responsible for mind-wandering, daydreaming, and self-referential thinking. While the DMN is essential for creativity and introspection, it can also hinder productivity.

When the DMN is active during work tasks, it can lead to distractions and decreased focus. To improve productivity, it is important to activate the task-positive network (TPN), which is responsible for focused attention and goal-directed behavior.

There are several ways to activate the TPN and reduce the activity of the DMN. One effective method is mindfulness meditation. By practicing mindfulness, we can train our brains to stay present and focused on the task at hand. Other techniques include setting clear goals, breaking tasks into smaller manageable chunks, and eliminating distractions such as social media or email notifications.

The Role of Dopamine in Motivation and Productivity

Dopamine is a neurotransmitter that plays a crucial role in motivation and reward. It is often referred to as the "feel-good" chemical because it is released when we experience pleasure or achieve a goal. Dopamine is also involved in regulating attention, focus, and decision-making.

To boost productivity, it is important to increase dopamine levels in the brain. One way to do this is by setting achievable goals and rewarding yourself when you accomplish them. This can create a positive feedback loop that motivates you to continue working towards your objectives.

Another way to increase dopamine levels is through exercise. Physical activity has been shown to release dopamine in the brain, leading to improved mood and increased motivation. Additionally, engaging in activities that you enjoy and find fulfilling can also boost dopamine levels and enhance productivity.

The Science of Procrastination: Why We Delay and How to Overcome It

Procrastination is a common phenomenon that affects many people's productivity. It is the act of delaying or postponing tasks, often in favor of more pleasurable or easier activities. While procrastination may provide temporary relief, it can have negative consequences on our productivity and overall well-being.

The science behind procrastination lies in the brain's reward system. When we engage in pleasurable activities such as watching TV or scrolling through social media, our brain releases dopamine, which reinforces the behavior. This can make it difficult to resist immediate gratification and prioritize long-term goals.

To overcome procrastination, it is important to understand the underlying reasons for delaying tasks. This could be due to fear of failure, perfectionism, or feeling overwhelmed by the magnitude of the task. Once you identify the root cause of your procrastination, you can develop strategies to address it.

Some effective strategies for overcoming procrastination include breaking tasks into smaller, more manageable steps, setting deadlines for each step, and using tools such as timers or productivity apps to stay on track. It can also be helpful to create a supportive environment by eliminating distractions and seeking accountability from a friend or colleague.

The Power of Habits: How to Form Good Ones and Break Bad Ones

Habits play a significant role in our productivity. They are automatic behaviors that we perform without conscious thought, allowing us to conserve mental energy and focus on more complex tasks. However, not all habits are beneficial for productivity.

To improve productivity, it is important to form good habits and break bad ones. Good habits can include setting a consistent schedule, prioritizing tasks, and practicing self-discipline. Breaking bad habits may involve identifying triggers and finding alternative behaviors to replace them.

One effective strategy for forming good habits is the habit loop, which consists of three components: the cue, the routine, and the reward. By identifying the cue that triggers a habit, you can consciously choose a new routine that aligns with your productivity goals. Additionally, rewarding yourself after completing a habit can reinforce the behavior and make it more likely to stick.

Breaking bad habits can be more challenging, as they are often deeply ingrained in our routines. However, by replacing the routine with a healthier alternative and being mindful of the triggers that lead to the habit, it is possible to break free from unproductive behaviors.

The Impact of Multitasking on Productivity and Brain Functioning

Multitasking is often seen as a desirable skill in today's fast-paced world. However, research has shown that multitasking can actually decrease productivity and impair brain functioning.

When we multitask, our attention becomes divided between multiple tasks, leading to decreased focus and increased errors. Additionally, switching between tasks can result in a cognitive cost known as "switching time," where our brains need time to refocus on the new task.

To improve productivity, it is important to avoid multitasking and instead focus on one task at a time. This allows us to give our full attention to the task at hand and complete it more efficiently. It can also reduce stress levels and improve the quality of our work.

One effective strategy for avoiding multitasking is to prioritize tasks and allocate dedicated time blocks for each one. By creating a schedule and sticking to it, you can ensure that you have uninterrupted time to focus on important tasks. Additionally, eliminating distractions such as phone notifications or email alerts can help maintain focus and prevent multitasking.

The Benefits of Taking Breaks: How to Optimize Your Rest Time

Taking breaks is essential for maintaining productivity and preventing burnout. Research has shown that regular breaks can improve focus, creativity, and overall well-being.

When we work for extended periods without breaks, our attention and cognitive resources become depleted, leading to decreased productivity and increased errors. Taking short breaks throughout the day allows our brains to recharge and replenish these resources, leading to improved performance.

To optimize rest time, it is important to engage in activities that promote relaxation and rejuvenation. This could include going for a walk, practicing deep breathing exercises, or engaging in a hobby or leisure activity. Additionally, incorporating mindfulness practices during breaks can help reduce stress levels and improve focus.

It is also important to schedule regular longer breaks, such as lunch breaks or vacation time. These extended periods of rest allow us to fully disconnect from work and recharge both physically and mentally. By prioritizing rest and relaxation, we can maintain high levels of productivity and prevent burnout.

The Science of Sleep: How it Affects Your Productivity and Brain Health

Sleep plays a crucial role in our productivity and overall brain health. It is during sleep that our brains consolidate memories, process information, and restore energy levels.

Lack of sleep can have detrimental effects on productivity. It impairs cognitive function, attention, and decision-making abilities. Additionally, chronic sleep deprivation has been linked to an increased risk of mental health disorders such as depression and anxiety.

To improve productivity, it is important to prioritize sleep and establish a consistent sleep routine. This includes going to bed and waking up at the same time each day, creating a sleep-friendly environment, and practicing relaxation techniques before bed.

Additionally, practicing good sleep hygiene can help improve the quality of your sleep. This includes avoiding caffeine and stimulating activities before bed, limiting exposure to screens, and creating a relaxing bedtime routine.

The Importance of Mindfulness: How to Stay Focused and Calm

Mindfulness is the practice of being fully present and aware of the present moment. It has been shown to improve focus, reduce stress levels, and enhance overall well-being.

In today's fast-paced world, it can be challenging to stay focused and calm. Our minds are often filled with thoughts about the past or worries about the future. However, by practicing mindfulness, we can train our brains to stay present and focused on the task at hand.

There are several ways to incorporate mindfulness into your daily routine. This could include practicing meditation, engaging in mindful breathing exercises, or simply taking a few moments throughout the day to pause and observe your surroundings.

By cultivating a mindfulness practice, you can improve your ability to stay focused, reduce stress levels, and enhance your overall productivity.

The Role of Nutrition and Exercise in Boosting Productivity

Nutrition and exercise play a significant role in our productivity. A healthy diet and regular physical activity can provide us with the energy and mental clarity needed to perform at our best.

Eating a balanced diet that includes whole foods, fruits, vegetables, lean proteins, and healthy fats can provide us with the nutrients needed for optimal brain function. Additionally, staying hydrated throughout the day is essential for maintaining cognitive function and preventing fatigue.

Regular exercise has been shown to improve cognitive function, memory, and overall mood. It increases blood flow to the brain, stimulates the release of endorphins (feel-good hormones), and reduces stress levels. Incorporating physical activity into your daily routine, such as going for a walk or practicing yoga, can help boost productivity and enhance overall well-being.

Applying the Science of Productivity to Your Work Habits

In conclusion, productivity is crucial for personal and professional success in today's fast-paced world. By understanding the science behind productivity and implementing strategies to improve focus, motivation, and well-being, we can make the most of our time and achieve our goals.

Some key takeaways from this article include:

- Activating the task-positive network and reducing the activity of the default mode network to improve focus and productivity.

- Increasing dopamine levels through goal-setting, rewarding yourself, and engaging in activities you enjoy.

- Overcoming procrastination by understanding the underlying reasons for delaying tasks and implementing strategies such as breaking tasks into smaller steps and seeking accountability.

- Forming good habits and breaking bad ones through the habit loop and mindful awareness of triggers.

- Avoiding multitasking and focusing on one task at a time to improve productivity and reduce cognitive load.

- Taking regular breaks to recharge and optimize rest time.

- Prioritizing sleep and practicing good sleep hygiene to improve productivity and brain health.

- Cultivating mindfulness to stay focused, reduce stress levels, and enhance overall well-being.

- Nourishing your body with a balanced diet and engaging in regular physical activity to boost energy levels and cognitive function.

By applying these strategies to your work habits, you can prioritize productivity, achieve your goals, and lead a more fulfilling life. Remember that productivity is not about working harder; it's about working smarter and making the most of your time.

Chapter: 16: Challenges

Challenges are obstacles or difficulties that individuals or organizations face in their personal and professional lives. They can come in various forms and can be both internal and external. Challenges are an inherent part of life and play a crucial role in personal and professional growth.

They push individuals and organizations out of their comfort zones, forcing them to adapt, learn, and develop new skills.

Challenges are important because they provide opportunities for growth and development. They push individuals to step outside of their comfort zones and confront their fears and limitations. By facing challenges head-on, individuals can develop resilience, problem-solving skills, and self-confidence. Similarly, organizations that embrace challenges can innovate, improve their processes, and stay competitive in the market.

Common Challenges Faced by Individuals and Organizations

1. Personal Challenges:

Personal challenges are obstacles that individuals face in their personal lives. These challenges can vary from person to person but there are some common ones that many people encounter. One common personal challenge is time management. Balancing work, family, and personal commitments can be overwhelming, leading to stress and a lack of productivity. Another personal challenge is self-doubt. Many individuals struggle with self-confidence and may doubt their abilities or worthiness of success. Fear of failure is another personal challenge that can hold individuals back from taking risks or pursuing their goals.

2. Organizational Challenges:

Organizational challenges are obstacles that businesses and other organizations face in their operations. These challenges can have a significant impact on the success or failure of the organization. One common organizational challenge is competition. In today's globalized world, organizations face intense competition from both domestic and international competitors. Financial constraints are another common organizational challenge. Limited resources can restrict an organization's ability to invest in new technologies, hire talented employees, or expand its operations. Employee turnover is another organizational challenge that can disrupt productivity and hinder growth.

Overcoming Personal Challenges: Strategies for Success

1. Setting realistic goals:

Setting realistic goals is essential for overcoming personal challenges. By setting achievable and measurable goals, individuals can stay focused and motivated. It is important to break down larger goals into smaller, manageable tasks to avoid feeling overwhelmed. Celebrating small wins along the way can also provide a sense of accomplishment and motivation.

2. Developing a growth mindset:

A growth mindset is the belief that abilities and intelligence can be developed through dedication and hard work. By adopting a growth mindset, individuals can view challenges as opportunities for learning and growth rather than as threats. This mindset allows individuals to embrace failure as a stepping stone to success and encourages them to persist in the face of obstacles.

3. Seeking support from others:

Seeking support from others is crucial in overcoming personal challenges. This can include seeking advice from mentors or trusted friends, joining support groups or communities, or seeking professional help if needed. Having a support system can provide encouragement, guidance, and accountability.

4. Practicing self-care:

Taking care of oneself is essential in overcoming personal challenges. This includes getting enough sleep, eating a balanced diet, exercising regularly, and engaging in activities that bring joy and relaxation. Self-care helps individuals maintain physical and mental well-being, which in turn enhances their ability to face challenges.

Dealing with Professional Challenges: Tips and Tricks

1. Identifying the root cause of the challenge:

To effectively overcome professional challenges, it is important to identify the root cause of the challenge. This involves analyzing the situation, gathering information, and understanding the underlying factors contributing to the challenge. By identifying the root cause, individuals can develop targeted strategies to address the challenge.

2. Seeking feedback and advice from colleagues:

Seeking feedback and advice from colleagues can provide valuable insights and perspectives on how to overcome professional challenges. Colleagues who have faced similar challenges may have valuable experiences and strategies to share. Additionally, seeking feedback from supervisors or mentors can help individuals gain a better understanding of their strengths and areas for improvement.

3. Developing a plan of action:

Developing a plan of action is crucial in overcoming professional challenges. This involves setting clear goals, outlining the steps needed to achieve those goals, and creating a timeline for completion. A well-thought-out plan provides structure and direction, making it easier to navigate through the challenge.

4. Staying adaptable and flexible:

Professional challenges often require individuals to adapt and be flexible in their approach. This may involve adjusting strategies, exploring alternative solutions, or being open to new ideas. Staying adaptable and flexible allows individuals to respond effectively to changing circumstances and find innovative solutions to challenges.

The Role of Challenges in Personal Growth and Development

1. How challenges can lead to increased resilience and self-confidence:

Challenges provide opportunities for individuals to develop resilience and self-confidence. By facing and overcoming challenges, individuals learn that they are capable of handling difficult situations and that setbacks are temporary. This builds resilience, which is the ability to bounce back from adversity. Similarly, successfully overcoming challenges boosts self-confidence and belief in one's abilities.

2. The importance of learning from failures and setbacks:

Failures and setbacks are inevitable when facing challenges. However, these experiences provide valuable lessons and opportunities for growth. By reflecting on failures and setbacks, individuals can identify areas for improvement, learn from their mistakes, and develop new strategies for success. Learning from failures is an essential part of personal growth and development.

3. The benefits of stepping outside of one's comfort zone:

Stepping outside of one's comfort zone is necessary for personal growth and development. Comfort zones are familiar and safe but they also limit growth and prevent individuals from reaching their full potential. By embracing challenges that push them outside of their comfort zones, individuals can develop new skills, gain new experiences, and expand their capabilities.

Turning Challenges into Opportunities: A Positive Mindset

1. The power of reframing challenges as opportunities:

Reframing challenges as opportunities is a powerful mindset shift that can change how individuals approach and overcome challenges. Instead of viewing challenges as obstacles or threats, individuals can see them as opportunities for growth, learning, and development. This positive mindset allows individuals to approach challenges with optimism and creativity.

2. How a positive attitude can lead to creative problem-solving:

A positive attitude is essential in creative problem-solving. When faced with a challenge, individuals with a positive attitude are more likely to approach the problem with an open mind, explore different perspectives, and think outside the box. This mindset allows for innovative and creative solutions to emerge.

3. The benefits of embracing change and uncertainty:

Challenges often involve change and uncertainty. Embracing change and uncertainty allows individuals to adapt quickly, be flexible in their approach, and find new opportunities within the challenge. By embracing change, individuals can navigate through challenges more effectively and discover new possibilities for growth.

How to Stay Motivated When Facing Challenges

1. Setting short-term and long-term goals:

Setting both short-term and long-term goals provides individuals with a sense of direction and purpose when facing challenges. Short-term goals provide immediate motivation and a sense of progress, while long-term goals provide a vision for the future. By setting goals, individuals can stay motivated and focused on overcoming challenges.

2. Celebrating small wins along the way:

Celebrating small wins along the way is important in maintaining motivation when facing challenges. Recognizing and celebrating progress, no matter how small, provides a sense of accomplishment and boosts motivation. This positive reinforcement encourages individuals to continue working towards their goals.

3. Finding inspiration and motivation from others:

Finding inspiration and motivation from others can be a powerful tool in overcoming challenges. This can include reading success stories, listening to motivational speeches or podcasts, or surrounding oneself with positive and supportive individuals. Drawing inspiration from others who have faced and overcome similar challenges can provide encouragement and motivation.

4. Practicing self-compassion and forgiveness:

Practicing self-compassion and forgiveness is important when facing challenges. It is natural to make mistakes or experience setbacks along the way. Instead of being self-critical or dwelling on failures, individuals should practice self-compassion and forgive themselves for their shortcomings. This allows individuals to learn from their mistakes and move forward with renewed motivation.

The Importance of Perseverance When Overcoming Challenges

1. The role of persistence in achieving success:

Persistence is key in overcoming challenges and achieving success. Challenges often require time, effort, and perseverance to overcome. By staying committed to their goals and persisting in the face of obstacles, individuals increase their chances of success.

2. How to stay committed to one's goals:

Staying committed to one's goals requires discipline and determination. One way to stay committed is by regularly reviewing and reminding oneself of the reasons why the goal is important. Breaking down the goal into smaller, manageable tasks can also help maintain motivation and commitment.

3. The benefits of learning from failures and setbacks:

Failures and setbacks are inevitable when facing challenges. However, these experiences provide valuable lessons and opportunities for growth. By reflecting on failures and setbacks, individuals can identify areas for improvement, learn from their mistakes, and develop new strategies for success. Learning from failures is an essential part of personal growth and development.

Addressing Challenges in Teamwork: Communication and Collaboration

1. The importance of open and honest communication:

Open and honest communication is crucial in addressing challenges in teamwork. It allows team members to express their thoughts, concerns, and ideas openly, fostering trust and collaboration. Effective communication ensures that everyone is on the same page and working towards a common goal.

2. Strategies for resolving conflicts and disagreements:

Conflicts and disagreements are common in teamwork, especially when facing challenges. It is important to address conflicts and disagreements promptly and constructively. This can be done by actively listening to all perspectives, finding common ground, and seeking win-win solutions. Mediation or facilitation may be necessary in more complex situations.

3. The benefits of working collaboratively towards a common goal:
Working collaboratively towards a common goal has numerous benefits when facing challenges. Collaboration allows team members to leverage their diverse skills, knowledge, and experiences to find innovative solutions. It fosters a sense of ownership and accountability among team members, leading to increased motivation and productivity.

The Impact of External Factors on Overcoming Challenges

1. How external factors can impact personal and professional challenges:
External factors such as economic downturns, global pandemics, or changes in regulations can have a significant impact on personal and professional challenges. These factors can create additional obstacles or constraints that individuals or organizations must navigate. It is important to recognize and adapt to these external factors when facing challenges.

2. Strategies for adapting to external challenges:
Adapting to external challenges requires flexibility and resilience. This may involve adjusting strategies, exploring new opportunities, or seeking alternative solutions. It is important to stay informed about external factors and their potential impact on personal or professional challenges.

3. The importance of staying resilient and adaptable:
Staying resilient and adaptable is crucial when facing external challenges. Resilience allows individuals or organizations to bounce back from adversity and find new ways forward. Adaptability enables individuals or organizations to adjust their strategies and approaches in response to changing circumstances.

Embracing Challenges as a Path to Success

In conclusion, challenges are an integral part of personal and professional growth. They provide opportunities for individuals and organizations to learn, develop new skills, and overcome obstacles. By adopting strategies such as setting realistic goals, developing a growth mindset, seeking support, and practicing self-care, individuals can overcome personal challenges. Similarly, by identifying the root cause of challenges, seeking feedback, developing a plan of action, and staying adaptable, organizations can overcome professional challenges. Challenges can lead to increased resilience, self-confidence, and personal growth. By reframing challenges as opportunities, embracing change and uncertainty, staying motivated, and practicing perseverance, individuals can turn challenges into stepping stones to success. Finally, addressing challenges in teamwork, adapting to external factors, and staying resilient are essential in overcoming challenges and achieving personal and professional goals.

Chapter 17: Navigating the Gig Economy: Pros and Cons of Freelancing

The gig economy and freelancing have become increasingly popular in recent years, as more and more people are seeking flexible work arrangements and the ability to be their own boss. The gig economy refers to a labor market characterized by the prevalence of short-term contracts or freelance work, as opposed to permanent jobs. Freelancing, on the other hand, is a form of self-employment where individuals offer their services on a project basis to multiple clients.

The concept of freelancing is not new; it has been around for centuries. However, with the advent of technology and the rise of the internet, freelancing has become more accessible and widespread. Today, anyone with a skill or expertise can become a freelancer and offer their services to clients all over the world.

Freelancing plays a crucial role in the modern economy. It provides individuals with the opportunity to earn a living doing what they love, while also giving businesses access to a diverse pool of talent. Freelancers are often hired for their specialized skills and can bring fresh perspectives and innovative ideas to projects. Additionally, freelancing allows companies to scale their workforce up or down as needed, without the long-term commitment of hiring full-time employees.

Pros of Freelancing: Flexibility and Autonomy

One of the biggest advantages of freelancing is the flexibility it offers. As a freelancer, you have the freedom to work from anywhere in the world. Whether you prefer working from home, a coffee shop, or while traveling, you have the ability to choose your own workspace. This flexibility allows you to create a work environment that suits your needs and preferences.

Another benefit of freelancing is the ability to set your own schedule. Unlike traditional 9-to-5 jobs, freelancers have the autonomy to decide when they want to work. This means you can work during your most productive hours, take breaks when needed, and have more control over your work-life balance. Freelancing also allows you to take time off whenever you need it, without having to ask for permission from a boss.

Freelancers also have the freedom to choose their own clients and projects. This means you can work on projects that align with your interests and passions. As a freelancer, you have the ability to say no to projects that don't excite you or don't align with your values. This level of autonomy allows you to have a greater sense of fulfillment and satisfaction in your work.

Cons of Freelancing: Inconsistent Income and Lack of Benefits

While freelancing offers many advantages, it also comes with its fair share of challenges. One of the biggest drawbacks of freelancing is the inconsistent income. Unlike traditional jobs where you receive a steady paycheck, freelancers often experience fluctuations in their income. Some months may be extremely busy and lucrative, while others may be slow and financially challenging.

Another disadvantage of freelancing is the lack of benefits that come with traditional employment. As a freelancer, you are responsible for providing your own health insurance, retirement plans, and other benefits that are typically offered by employers. This can be costly and time-consuming to manage, especially for those who are just starting out in their freelance careers.

Additionally, freelancers need to take on the responsibility of managing their own taxes and finances. Unlike employees who have taxes automatically deducted from their paychecks, freelancers are responsible for calculating and paying their own taxes. This requires careful record-keeping and financial planning to ensure compliance with tax laws and regulations.

Finding Freelance Work: Tips and Strategies

Finding freelance work can be challenging, especially when starting out. However, there are several strategies that can help you land clients and build a successful freelance career.

One of the most effective ways to find freelance work is through networking. Building relationships with other freelancers and professionals in your industry can lead to referrals and job opportunities. Attend industry events, join online communities and groups, and reach out to potential clients directly to expand your network.

Another strategy is to use online job boards and freelance marketplaces. Websites like Upwork, Freelancer, and Fiverr connect freelancers with clients looking for their services. These platforms allow you to create a profile, showcase your skills and experience, and bid on projects that interest you.

Reaching out to potential clients directly can also be an effective way to find freelance work. Research companies or individuals who may need your services and send them a personalized pitch or proposal. This approach requires more effort and persistence, but it can lead to long-term client relationships and higher-paying projects.

Building a strong online presence is essential for finding freelance work. Create a professional website or portfolio that showcases your work, skills, and experience. Use social media platforms like LinkedIn, Twitter, and Instagram to promote your services and engage with potential clients. Having a strong online presence can help you stand out from the competition and attract clients who are looking for your specific expertise.

Building a Strong Freelance Portfolio: Best Practices

A strong freelance portfolio is essential for showcasing your skills and attracting clients. Here are some best practices for building a compelling portfolio:

1. Showcasing your best work: Choose your best projects and include them in your portfolio. Highlight the results you achieved for each project and explain the challenges you faced and how you overcame them.

2. Highlighting your skills and experience: Clearly communicate your skills and expertise in your portfolio. Explain how your unique abilities can benefit potential clients and solve their problems.

3. Including testimonials from satisfied clients: Ask your previous clients for testimonials that highlight their satisfaction with your work. Testimonials provide social proof and build trust with potential clients.

4. Keeping your portfolio up-to-date: Regularly update your portfolio with new projects, skills, and achievements. This shows potential clients that you are actively working and continuously improving your craft.

Setting Your Freelance Rates: How to Determine Your Worth

Setting your freelance rates can be challenging, especially when starting out. Here are some factors to consider when determining your worth:

1. Researching industry standards and rates: Research what other freelancers in your industry are charging for similar services. This will give you a benchmark to work from and ensure that you are pricing yourself competitively.

2. Considering your experience and skills: Take into account your level of experience and the value you bring to clients. If you have specialized skills or expertise, you can justify charging higher rates.

3. Factoring in your expenses and taxes: Calculate your expenses, such as software subscriptions, equipment, and overhead costs, and factor them into your rates. Additionally, consider the amount of taxes you will need to pay and adjust your rates accordingly.

4. Negotiating rates with clients: Be prepared to negotiate rates with clients, especially when starting out. Consider offering discounts for long-term projects or bulk work, but make sure that the rates are still fair and sustainable for you.

Managing Your Time and Productivity as a Freelancer

Managing your time and productivity is crucial for success as a freelancer. Here are some tips to help you stay focused and productive:

1. Creating a schedule and sticking to it: Set specific working hours and create a schedule that aligns with your most productive times of the day. Stick to this schedule as much as possible to establish a routine.

2. Avoiding distractions: Minimize distractions by creating a dedicated workspace, turning off notifications on your phone, and using productivity tools like website blockers or time-tracking apps.

3. Using productivity tools and apps: There are numerous productivity tools and apps available that can help you stay organized, manage tasks, track time, and collaborate with clients. Experiment with different tools to find what works best for you.

4. Taking breaks and avoiding burnout: It's important to take regular breaks to rest and recharge. Schedule short breaks throughout the day and take longer breaks for meals or exercise. Avoid overworking yourself and prioritize self-care to prevent burnout.

Networking and Marketing Yourself as a Freelancer

Networking and marketing yourself are essential for building a successful freelance career. Here are some strategies to help you network and promote your work:

1. Attending industry events and conferences: Attend conferences, workshops, and networking events in your industry to meet potential clients and collaborators. These events provide opportunities to showcase your expertise and make valuable connections.

2. Joining online communities and groups: Participate in online communities and groups related to your industry. Engage in discussions, share your knowledge, and offer help to others. This will help you build relationships and establish yourself as an expert in your field.

3. Using social media to promote your work: Utilize social media platforms like LinkedIn, Twitter, and Instagram to showcase your work, share industry insights, and engage with potential clients. Be consistent in posting valuable content that demonstrates your expertise.

4. Building relationships with clients and other freelancers: Cultivate strong relationships with your clients by providing

exceptional service, delivering high-quality work, and maintaining open lines of communication. Additionally, connect with other freelancers in your industry to collaborate on projects or refer clients to each other.

Legal Considerations for Freelancers: Taxes and Contracts

As a freelancer, it's important to understand the legal considerations that come with running your own business. Here are some key areas to consider:

1. Understanding tax laws and regulations: Familiarize yourself with the tax laws and regulations that apply to freelancers in your country or region. Consult with a tax professional if needed to ensure compliance and maximize deductions.

2. Creating contracts and agreements with clients: Use contracts and agreements to clearly outline the scope of work, payment terms, and other important details with your clients. This helps protect both parties and ensures that expectations are clear from the beginning.

3. Protecting your intellectual property: If you create original work, such as designs, writing, or software code, it's important to understand your rights and protect your intellectual property. Consider registering copyrights or trademarks if necessary.

4. Seeking legal advice when necessary: If you encounter legal issues or have concerns about contracts, intellectual property, or other legal matters, seek advice from a lawyer who specializes in freelance or small business law.

Balancing Freelance Work with Other Responsibilities

Balancing freelance work with other responsibilities can be challenging. Here are some tips to help you manage your time and maintain a healthy work-life balance:

1. Managing family and personal obligations: Communicate with your family and loved ones about your work schedule and commitments. Set boundaries and establish dedicated time for family and personal activities.

2. Maintaining a work-life balance: Prioritize self-care and make time for activities that bring you joy and relaxation. Set aside time for hobbies, exercise, and spending time with loved ones.

3. Setting boundaries and prioritizing tasks: Learn to say no to projects or commitments that don't align with your priorities or values. Set clear boundaries with clients and establish realistic deadlines to avoid overworking yourself.

4. Seeking support from friends and family: Reach out to friends, family, or fellow freelancers for support and advice. Having a support system can help you navigate the challenges of freelancing and provide a sense of community.

Is Freelancing Right for You?

Freelancing offers many benefits, such as flexibility, autonomy, and the ability to work on projects that interest you. However, it also comes with challenges like inconsistent income and the need to manage your own taxes and finances. Before deciding to become a freelancer, ask yourself the following questions:

- Do you have the discipline and self-motivation to work independently?

- Are you comfortable with the uncertainty of inconsistent income?

- Can you handle the responsibility of managing your own taxes and finances?

- Do you have a strong network or the ability to build one?

- Are you willing to continuously learn and adapt to changes in your industry?

If you answered yes to these questions, freelancing may be a good fit for you. However, it's important to carefully consider the pros and cons and make an informed decision. Freelancing can be a rewarding and fulfilling career path, but it requires dedication, perseverance, and a willingness to continuously learn and grow.

Chapter 17: Celebrating Neurodiversity: Embracing Differences in the Brain

Neurodiversity is a concept that recognizes and celebrates the natural variation in human neurological functioning. It encompasses a range of conditions, including autism, ADHD, dyslexia, and others. Rather than viewing these conditions as disorders or deficits, neurodiversity emphasizes the unique strengths and perspectives that neurodivergent individuals bring to society.

Understanding and embracing neurodiversity is crucial for creating inclusive communities that value and support all individuals. By recognizing the diversity of human neurological functioning, we can challenge stereotypes and promote a more accurate understanding of neurodivergent individuals. This article will explore the different types of neurodivergent conditions, the benefits of embracing neurodiversity in society, the importance of recognizing and accommodating neurodivergent individuals in the workplace, the role of education in supporting neurodivergent students, debunking common myths and stereotypes about neurodivergent individuals, the impact of neurodiversity on relationships and social interactions, celebrating the unique strengths and talents of neurodivergent individuals, promoting advocacy and empowerment for neurodivergent communities, and overcoming stigma and discrimination against neurodivergent individuals.

Understanding the Different Types of Neurodivergent Conditions

Neurodiversity encompasses a wide range of conditions, each with its own unique characteristics and challenges. Autism is one of the most well-known neurodivergent conditions. It is characterized by difficulties with social interaction, communication, and repetitive behaviors. Individuals on the autism spectrum often have strengths in areas such as pattern recognition, attention to detail, and problem-solving.

ADHD (Attention-Deficit/Hyperactivity Disorder) is another common neurodivergent condition. It is characterized by difficulties with attention, impulsivity, and hyperactivity. While individuals with ADHD may struggle with tasks that require sustained focus, they often excel in situations that require quick thinking and multitasking.

Dyslexia is a neurodivergent condition that affects reading and language processing. Individuals with dyslexia may have difficulty with reading, spelling, and writing, but they often have strengths in areas such as creativity, problem-solving, and visual thinking.

Each neurodivergent condition has its own unique set of challenges and strengths. By understanding these conditions and the experiences of neurodivergent individuals, we can create more inclusive and supportive communities.

The Benefits of Embracing Neurodiversity in Society

Embracing neurodiversity in society has numerous benefits. First and foremost, it contributes to human diversity. Just as we celebrate and value other forms of diversity, such as race, gender, and culture, we should also celebrate and value neurological diversity. Neurodivergent individuals bring unique perspectives, skills, and talents to the table, enriching our communities and fostering innovation.

Neurodiversity also challenges the notion that there is a "normal" or "typical" way of thinking or being. By recognizing that there are many different ways of experiencing the world, we can break down barriers and promote a more inclusive society. This not only benefits neurodivergent individuals but also benefits everyone by fostering creativity, problem-solving, and collaboration.

Creating inclusive communities that value neurodiversity is essential for ensuring that all individuals have equal opportunities to thrive. By embracing neurodiversity, we can create environments where neurodivergent individuals feel accepted, supported, and empowered to reach their full potential.

The Importance of Recognizing and Accommodating Neurodivergent Individuals in the Workplace

Recognizing and accommodating neurodivergent individuals in the workplace is not only the right thing to do but also has numerous benefits for employers. Neurodivergent individuals often possess unique skills and strengths that can be valuable assets to organizations. For example, individuals with autism may excel in tasks that require attention to detail, pattern recognition, and logical thinking. Individuals with ADHD may thrive in fast-paced environments that require multitasking and quick thinking.

By hiring neurodivergent individuals, organizations can tap into this pool of talent and benefit from the diverse perspectives and skills they bring. Research has shown that neurodivergent individuals can contribute to increased innovation, problem-solving, and creativity in the workplace.

Accommodating neurodivergent employees is also crucial for creating an inclusive and supportive work environment. Simple accommodations, such as providing clear instructions, allowing flexible work hours, or providing quiet spaces for concentration, can make a significant difference for neurodivergent individuals. By creating an environment that values and supports neurodiversity, organizations can foster a culture of inclusivity and improve employee satisfaction and productivity.

The Role of Education in Supporting Neurodivergent Students

Traditional education settings can present significant challenges for neurodivergent students. Many neurodivergent individuals may struggle with aspects of the traditional curriculum or have difficulty with social interactions in the classroom. It is essential for educators to recognize and address these challenges to create inclusive and supportive learning environments.

One strategy for supporting neurodivergent students is to provide individualized accommodations and support. This may include providing extra time for assignments or tests, offering alternative methods of assessment, or providing assistive technology. By tailoring the learning experience to meet the needs of neurodivergent students, educators can help them succeed academically and build confidence.

In addition to individualized accommodations, it is crucial to promote understanding and acceptance of neurodiversity among students and staff. This can be done through education and awareness programs that teach students about different neurodivergent conditions and promote empathy and inclusion. By fostering a culture of acceptance and understanding, schools can create an environment where all students feel valued and supported.

Debunking Common Myths and Stereotypes About Neurodivergent Individuals

Neurodivergent individuals often face misconceptions and stereotypes that can lead to stigma and discrimination. It is essential to challenge these myths and promote a more accurate understanding of neurodivergent individuals.

One common myth is that neurodivergent individuals are less intelligent or capable than their neurotypical peers. In reality, neurodivergent individuals often have unique strengths and talents that can be valuable assets in various domains. For example, individuals with autism may excel in areas such as mathematics, music, or visual arts. By recognizing and celebrating these strengths, we can challenge the misconception that neurodivergent individuals are less capable.

Another myth is that neurodivergent individuals lack empathy or social skills. While it is true that some neurodivergent individuals may struggle with social interactions, this does not mean they lack empathy or the ability to form meaningful relationships. By promoting understanding and providing support, we can help neurodivergent individuals navigate social interactions and build positive relationships.

Challenging stereotypes and promoting accurate understanding is crucial for creating inclusive communities that value and support neurodiversity.

The Impact of Neurodiversity on Relationships and Social Interactions

Neurodivergent individuals may experience and navigate social interactions differently than their neurotypical peers. For example, individuals with autism may struggle with nonverbal communication or have difficulty understanding social cues. Individuals with ADHD may have challenges with impulse control or maintaining focus during conversations.

It is important to recognize and respect these differences in social interactions. Rather than expecting neurodivergent individuals to conform to neurotypical norms, we should strive to create inclusive environments where all individuals feel accepted and understood.

Building positive relationships with neurodivergent individuals requires patience, empathy, and open-mindedness. It is important to listen actively, be nonjudgmental, and provide clear communication. By creating a safe and supportive space for neurodivergent individuals to express themselves, we can foster meaningful connections and promote social inclusion.

Celebrating the Unique Strengths and Talents of Neurodivergent Individuals

Neurodivergent individuals possess unique strengths and talents that should be recognized and celebrated. For example, individuals with autism often have exceptional attention to detail, pattern recognition, and problem-solving skills. Individuals with ADHD may excel in tasks that require quick thinking, multitasking, and adaptability. Individuals with dyslexia may have strengths in areas such as creativity, visual thinking, and problem-solving.

By recognizing and celebrating these strengths, we can challenge the notion that neurodivergent individuals are "broken" or "deficient." Instead, we can promote a more accurate understanding of neurodiversity as a natural variation in human neurological functioning.

Celebrating the unique strengths and talents of neurodivergent individuals also benefits society as a whole. By tapping into these strengths, we can foster innovation, creativity, and problem-solving in various domains. Whether it is in the arts, sciences, technology, or other fields, neurodivergent individuals have the potential to make significant contributions to society.

Promoting Advocacy and Empowerment for Neurodivergent Communities

Promoting self-advocacy and empowerment is crucial for supporting neurodivergent individuals and communities. By empowering neurodivergent individuals to speak up for their needs and rights, we can help them navigate systems and advocate for necessary accommodations and support.

One strategy for promoting advocacy is to provide education and resources that empower neurodivergent individuals to understand their rights and self-advocate effectively. This may include workshops or training programs that teach self-advocacy skills, as well as resources that provide information on legal rights and available support services.

In addition to individual advocacy, it is important to support and promote neurodivergent communities. By creating spaces where neurodivergent individuals can connect, share experiences, and support one another, we can foster a sense of belonging and empowerment. This can be done through community organizations, support groups, or online platforms that provide a safe and inclusive space for neurodivergent individuals to come together.

Overcoming Stigma and Discrimination Against Neurodivergent Individuals

Neurodivergent individuals often face stigma and discrimination due to misconceptions and stereotypes. This can have a significant impact on their well-being and quality of life. It is crucial to challenge and overcome stigma and discrimination to create a more inclusive society.

One strategy for overcoming stigma is to promote education and awareness about neurodiversity. By providing accurate information about different neurodivergent conditions and challenging misconceptions, we can promote understanding and empathy. This can be done through public awareness campaigns, educational programs in schools, or media representation that portrays neurodivergent individuals in a positive and accurate light.

Another strategy is to advocate for policies and practices that promote inclusion and equal opportunities for neurodivergent individuals. This may include advocating for anti-discrimination laws, promoting accessible environments, or encouraging employers to adopt inclusive hiring practices.

By challenging stigma and discrimination, we can create a society that values and supports all individuals, regardless of their neurological differences.

Embracing Neurodiversity as a Vital Part of Human Diversity

In conclusion, understanding and embracing neurodiversity is crucial for creating inclusive communities that value and support all individuals. Neurodiversity encompasses a range of conditions, each with its own unique characteristics and challenges. By recognizing the diversity of human neurological functioning, we can challenge stereotypes, promote accurate understanding, and celebrate the unique strengths and talents of neurodivergent individuals.

Embracing neurodiversity has numerous benefits for society. It contributes to human diversity, fosters innovation and creativity, and promotes a more inclusive and equitable society. By recognizing and accommodating neurodivergent individuals in the workplace, supporting neurodivergent students in education settings, challenging myths and stereotypes, promoting positive relationships and social interactions, celebrating unique strengths and talents, promoting advocacy and empowerment, and overcoming stigma and discrimination, we can create a society that values and supports neurodiversity as a vital part of human diversity.

It is essential for individuals, communities, organizations, and policymakers to take action to embrace and celebrate neurodiversity. By doing so, we can create a more inclusive and equitable society where all individuals have equal opportunities to thrive.

Chapter 18: The Benefits of Inclusion

Inclusion is the act of including or involving everyone, regardless of their differences or backgrounds. It is about creating a society where everyone feels valued, respected, and supported. Inclusion is not just a buzzword; it is a fundamental aspect of a thriving and harmonious society. It is about recognizing and embracing diversity in all its forms, including race, ethnicity, gender, age, disability, sexual orientation, and more. Inclusion is crucial because it promotes equality, fosters innovation, and creates a sense of belonging for all individuals.

The Business Case for Inclusion

Inclusion is not only a moral imperative but also a smart business decision. Numerous studies have shown that companies that prioritize diversity and inclusion outperform their competitors. When organizations embrace inclusion, they benefit from increased productivity and profitability. This is because diverse teams bring different perspectives and ideas to the table, leading to more innovative solutions and better decision-making.

Moreover, inclusive companies tend to have higher customer satisfaction rates. When customers see themselves represented in the products or services they use, they feel understood and valued. This leads to increased loyalty and positive word-of-mouth recommendations.

Additionally, by embracing inclusion, companies gain access to a wider talent pool. When organizations are open to hiring individuals from diverse backgrounds, they can attract top talent from all walks of life. This not only brings fresh perspectives and ideas but also helps create a more inclusive workforce that reflects the diversity of their customer base.

The Social Benefits of Inclusion

Inclusion plays a vital role in creating a more diverse and accepting community. When individuals from different backgrounds come together and interact with one another, it breaks down barriers and fosters understanding. This leads to reduced discrimination and prejudice as people learn to appreciate and respect each other's differences.

Furthermore, inclusion helps create a society where everyone feels valued and included. When individuals feel accepted for who they are, it improves their overall well-being and mental health. Inclusive communities are more likely to have lower rates of social isolation and higher levels of happiness and satisfaction.

The Personal Benefits of Inclusion

Inclusion has significant personal benefits for individuals as well. When people feel included, they experience improved mental health and well-being. They feel a sense of belonging and acceptance, which can help reduce stress, anxiety, and depression.

Moreover, inclusion boosts individuals' self-worth and self-esteem. When people are valued for their unique qualities and contributions, it enhances their confidence and empowers them to reach their full potential. Inclusive environments provide individuals with the support and encouragement they need to thrive personally and professionally.

The Importance of Inclusive Leadership

Inclusive leadership is crucial for creating a culture of acceptance and respect within organizations. Leaders play a pivotal role in setting the tone for inclusivity by modeling inclusive behaviors and values. When leaders prioritize diversity and inclusion, it sends a powerful message to employees that everyone's voice matters.

Inclusive leaders also create an environment where individuals feel safe to express their ideas and opinions without fear of judgment or discrimination. This fosters creativity, collaboration, and innovation within teams.

The Role of Diversity and Inclusion in Innovation

Diversity and inclusion are essential for driving innovation within organizations. When teams consist of individuals from diverse backgrounds, they bring different perspectives, experiences, and ideas to the table. This diversity of thought leads to more creative problem-solving and breakthrough innovations.

Furthermore, diverse teams are better equipped to understand the needs and preferences of a diverse customer base. This enables organizations to develop products and services that cater to a wider range of customers, leading to increased market share and competitive advantage.

Overcoming Barriers to Inclusion

While inclusion is crucial, there are often barriers that prevent its full realization. Bias and stereotypes in the workplace can hinder the progress towards creating an inclusive environment. It is essential for organizations to address these biases head-on and provide training and education to employees to raise awareness and promote understanding.

Additionally, organizations should implement policies and practices that promote diversity and inclusion. This includes creating diverse hiring panels, implementing inclusive language in job descriptions, and providing equal opportunities for career advancement.

Best Practices for Creating an Inclusive Workplace

Creating an inclusive workplace requires a concerted effort from both employers and employees. Employers can start by fostering a safe and welcoming environment where individuals feel comfortable being their authentic selves. This can be achieved through diversity training, employee resource groups, and mentorship programs.

Employees can contribute to creating an inclusive workplace by actively listening to their colleagues, challenging their own biases, and treating everyone with respect and dignity. It is important for individuals to educate themselves about different cultures, backgrounds, and perspectives to foster a more inclusive environment.

The Impact of Inclusion on Employee Engagement and Retention

Inclusion has a significant impact on employee engagement and retention. When individuals feel included and valued in the workplace, they are more likely to be engaged and committed to their work. They feel a sense of loyalty towards the organization and are motivated to contribute their best efforts.

Moreover, inclusive workplaces have lower turnover rates. When employees feel supported and included, they are less likely to seek opportunities elsewhere. This leads to cost savings for organizations in terms of recruitment, onboarding, and training.

Inclusion in the Digital Age

In today's digital age, technology can play a crucial role in bridging the gap and promoting inclusion. Technology has the power to connect people from different backgrounds and enable them to collaborate regardless of their physical location.

Furthermore, it is essential for organizations to ensure that their digital platforms are accessible to all individuals, including those with disabilities. This includes providing alternative text for images, closed captions for videos, and screen reader compatibility.

Inclusion is not just a nice-to-have; it is a necessity for a brighter and more equitable future. Embracing inclusion in all aspects of society, including business, social, and personal settings, is crucial for creating a more diverse, accepting, and harmonious world.

By prioritizing inclusion, organizations can reap the benefits of increased productivity, profitability, and customer satisfaction. Inclusive communities foster understanding and reduce discrimination and prejudice. On an individual level, inclusion improves mental health, well-being, and self-worth.

Inclusive leadership is essential for creating a culture of acceptance and respect within organizations. Diversity and inclusion drive innovation by bringing different perspectives to the table. Overcoming barriers to inclusion requires addressing bias and stereotypes in the workplace and providing training and education.

Creating an inclusive workplace requires effort from both employers and employees. Inclusion has a significant impact on employee engagement and retention. In the digital age, technology can help bridge the gap and ensure accessibility for all.

In conclusion, embracing inclusion is not only the right thing to do but also the smart thing to do. By encouraging others to embrace inclusion, we can create a more inclusive society that benefits everyone.

Chapter 19: The Power of Neurodivergent Thinking

Neurodivergent thinking refers to the cognitive processes and perspectives of individuals with neurodivergent conditions such as autism, ADHD, dyslexia, and others. It is a term that recognizes and embraces the diversity of human minds and challenges the notion that there is a single "normal" way of thinking. Neurodivergent individuals often have unique strengths and abilities that can contribute to problem-solving, creativity, innovation, and addressing societal challenges.

Neurodivergent conditions are characterized by differences in brain structure and function, which can result in atypical patterns of thinking, learning, and processing information. For example, individuals with autism may have heightened sensory perception and attention to detail, while those with ADHD may have difficulty with sustained attention but excel in multitasking. Dyslexic individuals may have difficulties with reading and writing but possess exceptional spatial reasoning skills.

Understanding and embracing neurodiversity is crucial for creating an inclusive society that values the contributions of all individuals. By recognizing the strengths and abilities of neurodivergent thinkers, we can foster environments that allow them to thrive and make valuable contributions to various fields.

The Benefits of Neurodivergent Thinking in Problem-Solving

Neurodivergent thinkers bring unique perspectives and approaches to problem-solving that can be highly valuable in various contexts. Their atypical patterns of thinking allow them to see connections and patterns that others may miss. This ability to think outside the box can lead to innovative solutions to complex problems.

For example, individuals with autism often excel in pattern recognition and attention to detail. They may notice patterns or anomalies that others overlook, which can be particularly useful in fields such as data analysis, quality control, or cybersecurity. Their ability to focus intensely on specific tasks or topics can also lead to deep insights and breakthroughs.

Furthermore, neurodivergent thinkers often have a high degree of creativity and divergent thinking. They can approach problems from unconventional angles and come up with novel solutions. This creative problem-solving can be particularly valuable in fields such as design, engineering, and entrepreneurship.

How Neurodivergent Thinkers Can Excel in the Workplace

Neurodivergent individuals have unique strengths that can make them highly valuable employees in various industries. For example, their attention to detail and ability to hyperfocus can make them excellent programmers, data analysts, or researchers. Their ability to think outside the box and see patterns can also be advantageous in fields such as marketing, design, and innovation.

Accommodating neurodivergent employees in the workplace is crucial for harnessing their full potential. Providing flexible work arrangements, clear communication channels, and sensory-friendly environments can help create a supportive and inclusive workplace. Additionally, providing training and resources to help neurotypical colleagues understand and appreciate neurodivergent thinking can foster collaboration and innovation.

Recognizing the strengths of neurodivergent thinkers and creating inclusive workplaces not only benefits the individuals themselves but also leads to more diverse perspectives and better problem-solving outcomes for organizations.

The Importance of Recognizing and Supporting Neurodiversity

Stigmatizing neurodivergent individuals can have significant negative effects on their well-being and opportunities for success. Many neurodivergent individuals face discrimination, bullying, and exclusion due to their differences in thinking and behavior. This can lead to mental health issues, low self-esteem, and limited access to education and employment opportunities.

Embracing neurodiversity in society has numerous benefits. It promotes inclusivity, equality, and social justice by recognizing the value of all individuals regardless of their cognitive differences. It also fosters creativity, innovation, and problem-solving by incorporating diverse perspectives into decision-making processes.

To fully support neurodivergent individuals, there is a need for more research and understanding of neurodivergent conditions. This includes studying the strengths and challenges associated with different conditions, developing effective interventions and accommodations, and promoting awareness and acceptance in society.

Neurodivergent Thinking and Creativity

There is a strong link between neurodivergent thinking and creativity. Many famous creatives throughout history have been neurodivergent individuals who have made significant contributions to their respective fields.

For example, Albert Einstein, one of the greatest scientific minds of all time, is believed to have had traits associated with autism. His ability to think in abstract terms, visualize complex concepts, and challenge conventional wisdom led to groundbreaking discoveries in physics.

Temple Grandin, a renowned animal behavior expert and autism advocate, has used her unique perspective as an individual with autism to revolutionize the livestock industry. Her insights into animal behavior and her innovative designs for more humane handling systems have had a profound impact on the industry.

Neurodivergent individuals often possess a heightened ability to think divergently, make unusual connections, and approach problems from unconventional angles. These qualities are essential for creativity and can lead to breakthroughs in fields such as art, music, writing, and design.

The Role of Neurodivergent Thinking in Innovation and Invention

Throughout history, neurodivergent individuals have made significant contributions to innovation and invention. Their unique perspectives and ways of thinking have led to groundbreaking discoveries and advancements in various fields.

Nikola Tesla, a brilliant inventor and electrical engineer, is believed to have had traits associated with ADHD. His ability to hyperfocus on his work and think in abstract terms allowed him to develop numerous inventions that revolutionized the field of electricity.

Steve Jobs, the co-founder of Apple Inc., was known for his intense focus, attention to detail, and ability to think differently. These traits, often associated with neurodivergent thinking, played a crucial role in the development of iconic products such as the iPhone and the Macintosh computer.

Neurodivergent individuals have the potential to drive future innovation and invention by bringing their unique perspectives and approaches to problem-solving. By recognizing and supporting their contributions, we can foster a culture of innovation that benefits society as a whole.

How Neurodivergent Thinking Can Help Address Societal Challenges

Neurodivergent individuals have the potential to contribute to solving some of the most pressing societal challenges we face today. Their unique perspectives and ways of thinking can offer fresh insights and innovative solutions to complex problems.

For example, neurodivergent individuals may have a heightened sensitivity to environmental issues, making them valuable contributors to addressing climate change. Their attention to detail and ability to see patterns can also be beneficial in fields such as healthcare, where accurate diagnosis and treatment are crucial.

Furthermore, neurodivergent individuals often possess a strong sense of justice and empathy, which can drive them to address social issues such as poverty, inequality, and discrimination. Their ability to think outside the box and challenge conventional wisdom can lead to innovative approaches to these challenges.

Including neurodivergent perspectives in problem-solving for societal challenges is essential for ensuring that diverse voices are heard and that solutions are effective and inclusive.

The Challenges Neurodivergent Thinkers May Face in Traditional Education Systems

Traditional education systems often present challenges for neurodivergent individuals. These systems are typically designed with neurotypical learners in mind, which can result in limited accommodations and support for those with atypical patterns of thinking and learning.

Neurodivergent students may struggle with aspects of traditional education such as rigid schedules, large class sizes, sensory overload, and standardized testing. These challenges can lead to feelings of frustration, anxiety, and low self-esteem.

Labeling and stigmatizing neurodivergent students can also have significant negative effects on their educational experiences. It can reinforce stereotypes, limit opportunities for success, and create barriers to accessing appropriate accommodations and support.

The Need for Inclusive Education and Workplace Environments

Creating inclusive education and workplace environments is crucial for accommodating the needs of neurodivergent individuals and harnessing their full potential. Inclusive environments recognize and value the diversity of minds and provide accommodations and support that allow all individuals to thrive.

In education, inclusive environments involve flexible teaching methods, individualized learning plans, sensory-friendly classrooms, and supportive resources. They also involve promoting awareness and acceptance of neurodiversity among students, teachers, and parents.

In the workplace, inclusive environments involve providing reasonable accommodations, such as flexible work arrangements, clear communication channels, and sensory-friendly workspaces. They also involve promoting understanding and appreciation of neurodivergent thinking among colleagues and managers.

Creating inclusive environments benefits not only neurodivergent individuals but also all individuals. It fosters diversity, creativity, and innovation by incorporating diverse perspectives into decision-making processes. It also promotes empathy, understanding, and social justice by challenging stereotypes and promoting inclusivity.

Success Stories of Neurodivergent Thinkers Changing the World

There are numerous success stories of neurodivergent individuals who have made significant contributions to society. These individuals have overcome challenges associated with their neurodivergent conditions and have used their unique perspectives and abilities to make positive impacts on the world.

Greta Thunberg, a young climate activist with Asperger's syndrome, has become a global leader in the fight against climate change. Her ability to think differently and her unwavering determination have inspired millions of people around the world to take action.

Dan Aykroyd, a renowned actor, comedian, and writer, has openly discussed his diagnosis of Asperger's syndrome. His unique perspective and ability to think outside the box have contributed to his success in the entertainment industry.

These success stories highlight the potential for neurodivergent individuals to make significant contributions to various fields and drive positive change in society. By recognizing and supporting their unique abilities, we can create a more inclusive and equitable world.

The Future of Neurodivergent Thinking and Its Potential Impact on Society

Neurodivergent thinking has the potential to drive innovation, creativity, and positive change in society. By recognizing and embracing the diversity of human minds, we can create inclusive environments that value the contributions of all individuals.

Understanding and supporting neurodiversity is crucial for addressing societal challenges, fostering innovation, and promoting social justice. It requires recognizing the strengths and abilities of neurodivergent thinkers, providing accommodations and support, and challenging stereotypes and stigmas.

Continued research and understanding of neurodivergent conditions and thinking are essential for creating a more inclusive society. This includes studying the strengths and challenges associated with different conditions, developing effective interventions and accommodations, and promoting awareness and acceptance in all aspects of life.

By embracing neurodiversity, we can create a world that values the unique perspectives and abilities of all individuals, leading to a more innovative, creative, and inclusive society.

Chapter 20: 5 Unique Accommodations That Will Make Your Vacation Unforgettable

When it comes to vacations, many people are looking for unique and memorable experiences. Gone are the days of settling for a standard hotel room when there are so many extraordinary accommodations available. From treehouses to underwater hotels, there are countless options for those seeking a one-of-a-kind stay. In this article, we will explore some of the most unique vacation experiences around the world.

Treehouses

For those who have always dreamed of escaping into the treetops, staying in a treehouse is the perfect option. Treehouses offer a unique and adventurous experience, allowing guests to reconnect with nature and enjoy stunning views from above. There are treehouse accommodations available in various locations around the world, each offering its own charm and amenities.

One example of a treehouse accommodation is the Treehotel in Sweden. Located in the middle of a forest, this hotel offers several different treehouses, each with its own unique design and theme. From a mirrored cube to a UFO-shaped structure, guests can choose their preferred style and enjoy a truly unforgettable stay.

Underwater hotels

For those who want to take their vacation experience to new depths, underwater hotels offer an extraordinary opportunity to sleep with the fishes. These hotels are designed to provide guests with an immersive experience, allowing them to observe marine life up close while enjoying all the comforts of a luxury hotel room.

The technology and design behind underwater hotels are truly remarkable. These structures are built to withstand the pressure of the water and provide guests with breathtaking views of the underwater world. They often feature large windows or even entire walls made of glass, allowing guests to feel as though they are part of the ocean.

Glamping

For those who want to enjoy the great outdoors without sacrificing comfort, glamping is the perfect option. Glamping combines the best of camping and luxury travel, offering guests the opportunity to stay in luxurious tents or cabins while still being surrounded by nature.

Glamping destinations can be found all over the world, from national parks to private estates. These accommodations often feature amenities such as comfortable beds, private bathrooms, and even gourmet meals prepared by a personal chef. Whether you prefer to stay in a safari tent in Africa or a yurt in the mountains, glamping offers a unique and unforgettable experience.

Ice hotels

If you're looking for a truly unique and magical experience, staying in an ice hotel is sure to fulfill your dreams. These hotels are constructed entirely out of ice and snow, offering guests the opportunity to cozy up in a room made of frozen water.

The construction and maintenance of ice hotels are no small feat. Each year, these hotels are built from scratch using blocks of ice harvested from nearby frozen lakes or rivers. The rooms are then decorated with ice sculptures and intricate designs, creating a stunning and ethereal atmosphere. Despite the chilly temperatures, guests are provided with warm sleeping bags and blankets to ensure a comfortable stay.

Houseboats

For those who love the water, staying in a houseboat offers a unique and tranquil experience. Houseboats allow guests to float on the water and wake up to stunning views of lakes, rivers, or even oceans. These accommodations often feature all the comforts of home, including bedrooms, bathrooms, kitchens, and even outdoor decks.

Houseboat destinations can be found all over the world, from the canals of Amsterdam to the backwaters of Kerala in India. Some houseboats are stationary, while others can be rented for a cruise along scenic waterways. Whether you're looking for a peaceful retreat or an adventurous journey, staying in a houseboat is sure to provide a memorable experience.

Cave hotels

For those who want to experience the natural beauty of a cave while still enjoying modern amenities, cave hotels offer the perfect solution. These accommodations are built into natural caves or rock formations, providing guests with a unique and immersive experience.

Cave hotels can be found in various locations around the world, from the ancient cave dwellings of Cappadocia in Turkey to the stunning cliffs of Santorini in Greece. These hotels often feature luxurious amenities such as spa facilities, private pools, and panoramic views of the surrounding landscape. Staying in a cave hotel allows guests to feel connected to nature while still enjoying all the comforts of a luxury hotel.

Airstreams

For those who love to travel in style and comfort, staying in a vintage airstream trailer is the perfect option. Airstreams are iconic American trailers known for their sleek design and luxurious interiors. These trailers offer all the comforts of home, including comfortable beds, fully equipped kitchens, and even bathrooms.

The history of airstream travel dates back to the 1930s when Wally Byam first introduced these trailers to the world. Since then, they have become a symbol of adventure and freedom. Today, there are countless airstream parks and campgrounds where guests can rent these trailers for a unique and memorable vacation experience.

Castles

For those who have always dreamed of living like royalty, staying in a castle-turned-hotel is the perfect option. Castle hotels offer guests the opportunity to step back in time and experience the grandeur and elegance of a bygone era.

Castle hotel destinations can be found all over the world, from the rolling hills of Scotland to the picturesque countryside of France. These hotels often feature luxurious amenities such as fine dining restaurants, spa facilities, and even private gardens. Staying in a castle allows guests to immerse themselves in history while still enjoying all the comforts of a modern hotel.

Lighthouses

For those who love breathtaking ocean views and a sense of history, staying in a historic lighthouse is an unforgettable experience. Lighthouse hotels offer guests the opportunity to stay in a unique and iconic structure while enjoying panoramic views of the surrounding coastline.

Lighthouse hotel locations can be found in various coastal destinations around the world, from the rugged cliffs of Ireland to the sandy beaches of the United States. These accommodations often feature cozy bedrooms, charming living areas, and even private balconies or terraces. Staying in a lighthouse allows guests to experience the beauty of the ocean while still enjoying all the comforts of a luxury hotel.

When it comes to vacations, why settle for a boring hotel room when there are so many extraordinary accommodations available? From treehouses to underwater hotels, there are countless options for those seeking a unique and memorable experience. Whether you're looking to escape into the treetops, sleep with the fishes, or cozy up in a room made of ice, these accommodations offer something for everyone. So why not try something different on your next vacation and create memories that will last a lifetime?

Chapter 21: Why We All Need Support Systems and How to Build Them

A support system is a network of individuals who provide emotional, practical, and sometimes financial assistance to someone in need. It is a group of people who are there to offer guidance, encouragement, and help during challenging times. Having a support system is crucial because it provides a sense of belonging, validation, and security. It can make a significant difference in one's mental health and overall well-being.

The Importance of Having a Support System in Your Life

A support system is essential because it provides a sense of connection and belonging. Humans are social beings, and we thrive when we have meaningful relationships with others. Having a support system means having people who genuinely care about your well-being and are there to offer support when you need it most.

In times of crisis or difficulty, a support system can be a lifeline. Whether it's dealing with the loss of a loved one, going through a breakup, or facing a major life transition, having people who can provide emotional support and practical assistance can make all the difference. They can offer a listening ear, offer advice or guidance, and help you navigate through challenging situations.

How a Support System Can Improve Your Mental Health

Research has consistently shown that social support plays a crucial role in mental health. Having a strong support system can help reduce stress, anxiety, and depression. When we have people we can rely on and confide in, it helps us feel understood and validated. This sense of connection can alleviate feelings of loneliness and isolation, which are often associated with poor mental health.

Studies have also shown that individuals with strong social support systems tend to have better coping mechanisms when faced with stressors. They are more likely to engage in healthy behaviors such as exercise, seek professional help when needed, and practice self-care. Additionally, having people who believe in us and encourage us can boost our self-esteem and confidence.

The Benefits of Having a Diverse Support System

Having a diverse support system is important because it exposes us to different perspectives, experiences, and ideas. It allows us to broaden our horizons and gain new insights. When we surround ourselves with people from different backgrounds, cultures, and professions, we are more likely to challenge our own beliefs and grow as individuals.

A diverse support system also provides us with a range of resources and expertise. Each person in our support system brings their own unique skills and knowledge to the table. For example, a friend who is a great listener can provide emotional support, while a family member who is financially savvy can offer advice on budgeting and saving.

Examples of different types of people who can be part of your support system include family members, friends, colleagues, mentors, therapists, and online communities. Each of these individuals can provide different types of support depending on their strengths and areas of expertise.

The Different Types of Support Systems You Can Build

There are various types of support systems that you can build depending on your needs and preferences. Some common types include:

1. Family support system: This includes immediate family members such as parents, siblings, and children. They are often the first line of support during challenging times.

2. Friend support system: Friends are often the ones we turn to for emotional support and companionship. They can provide a listening ear, offer advice, and help us navigate through difficult situations.

3. Professional support system: This includes mentors, colleagues, and supervisors who can offer guidance and advice in our professional lives. They can help us navigate career decisions, provide feedback on our work, and offer networking opportunities.

4. Online support system: With the rise of social media and online communities, it is now possible to build a support system online. These communities can provide a sense of belonging and connection, especially for individuals who may not have access to a strong offline support system.

5. Community support system: This includes individuals within your community who can offer support and assistance. This can include neighbors, community leaders, or members of local organizations.

How to Identify the People Who Can Be Part of Your Support System

Identifying the people who can be part of your support system requires some reflection and self-awareness. It's important to consider the qualities you value in a supportive person and the type of support you need.

Some qualities to look for in a supportive person include:

- Empathy: A supportive person should be able to understand and relate to your experiences and emotions.

- Non-judgmental: They should be accepting and open-minded, allowing you to express yourself without fear of judgment.

- Trustworthy: You should feel comfortable confiding in them and trusting that they will keep your conversations confidential.

- Reliable: A supportive person should be dependable and available when you need them.

- Good listener: They should be able to actively listen and provide a safe space for you to share your thoughts and feelings.

Approaching someone to be part of your support system can be as simple as expressing your needs and asking for their support. It's important to communicate openly and honestly about what you are looking for in a support system and how they can help.

The Role of Communication in Building and Maintaining Support Systems

Communication is key in building and maintaining a support system. It's important to express your needs, boundaries, and expectations clearly to ensure that everyone is on the same page.

Effective communication involves active listening, empathy, and validation. It's important to listen attentively when someone is sharing their thoughts or feelings and respond with empathy and understanding. Validating their experiences can help them feel heard and supported.

It's also important to communicate your own needs and boundaries. Letting others know what you need from them in terms of support can help them understand how they can best assist you. Additionally, setting boundaries is crucial to ensure that your support system remains healthy and balanced.

How to Nurture Your Support System and Keep It Strong

Nurturing your support system involves investing time and effort into maintaining the relationships. It's important to show appreciation for the support you receive and reciprocate when possible.

One way to nurture your support system is by being there for others when they need support. Just as they have been there for you, it's important to offer a listening ear, provide encouragement, and help them when possible. This reciprocity strengthens the bond and creates a sense of mutual trust and support.

Maintaining a healthy balance in your support system is also crucial. It's important to recognize when you are relying too heavily on one person or neglecting other relationships. By diversifying your support system and spreading out your needs among different individuals, you can ensure that no one person feels overwhelmed or burdened.

The Pitfalls to Avoid When Building a Support System

When building a support system, it's important to be mindful of common pitfalls that can hinder its effectiveness. Some common mistakes to avoid include:

1. Relying too heavily on one person: Putting all your emotional needs on one person can create an unhealthy dynamic and put strain on the relationship. It's important to diversify your support system and spread out your needs among different individuals.

2. Ignoring toxic relationships: It's important to recognize toxic relationships and remove them from your support system. Toxic individuals can drain your energy, undermine your self-esteem, and hinder your progress.

3. Failing to set healthy boundaries: Setting healthy boundaries is crucial in maintaining a healthy support system. It's important to communicate your needs and expectations clearly and assertively.

How to Ask for Help from Your Support System

Asking for help from your support system can be challenging, but it's an important skill to develop. When asking for help, it's important to be specific about what you need and how others can assist you. This clarity helps others understand how they can best support you.

It's also important to express gratitude for the support you receive. Showing appreciation for the assistance you receive reinforces the bond and encourages others to continue offering their support.

The Role of Self-Care in Maintaining a Support System

Self-care is crucial in maintaining a support system. It's important to prioritize your own well-being and take care of yourself so that you can be there for others. This means setting aside time for activities that bring you joy, practicing self-compassion, and seeking professional help when needed.

Recognizing when you need to take a break from your support system is also important. It's okay to step back and take time for yourself when you are feeling overwhelmed or burnt out. Communicating your needs and boundaries to your support system can help them understand and respect your need for space.

The Long-Term Benefits of Having a Strong Support System

Having a strong support system can have long-term benefits on your mental health and overall well-being. It provides a sense of belonging, validation, and security that can improve your quality of life.

A strong support system can also help you achieve your goals. Whether it's pursuing a new career, starting a business, or making positive lifestyle changes, having people who believe in you and offer guidance can make all the difference.

Additionally, a support system can provide a sense of purpose and meaning in life. Knowing that there are people who care about you and are there to support you through thick and thin can give you the motivation and resilience to overcome challenges.

In conclusion, having a support system is crucial for our mental health and overall well-being. It provides us with a sense of connection, validation, and security during challenging times. Building and maintaining a strong support system requires effort, communication, and reciprocity. By diversifying our support system, setting healthy boundaries, and practicing self-care, we can reap the long-term benefits of having a strong support system in our lives. So, reach out to your loved ones, build meaningful connections, and remember that you don't have to face life's challenges alone.

Chapter 22: Navigating Relationships with ADHD: Tips for Building Strong Connections

Attention-deficit/hyperactivity disorder (ADHD) is a neurodevelopmental disorder that affects both children and adults. It is characterized by symptoms such as inattention, hyperactivity, and impulsivity. While ADHD can have a significant impact on various aspects of an individual's life, it can also have a profound effect on relationships. Understanding and addressing ADHD in relationships is crucial for maintaining healthy and fulfilling connections with partners, family members, friends, and social networks.

Understanding ADHD and its Impact on Relationships

ADHD is often associated with symptoms such as difficulty paying attention, forgetfulness, impulsivity, and hyperactivity. These symptoms can manifest in different ways and can vary from person to person. In relationships, these symptoms can have a significant impact on communication, trust, intimacy, emotions, impulsivity, and responsibilities.

Communication can be challenging in relationships where one or both partners have ADHD. The individual with ADHD may struggle with listening attentively, following conversations, or staying focused during discussions. This can lead to misunderstandings and frustration for both partners. Trust can also be affected as the symptoms of ADHD may cause the individual to forget commitments or responsibilities, leading to feelings of unreliability or inconsistency.

Intimacy can be impacted by ADHD as well. The symptoms of inattention and impulsivity can make it difficult for individuals with ADHD to be fully present in intimate moments or to engage in deep emotional connections. Emotions may also be affected by ADHD, with individuals experiencing heightened emotional reactivity or difficulty regulating their emotions.

Communication Strategies for Couples with ADHD

Clear and effective communication is essential for any relationship, but it becomes even more crucial when one or both partners have ADHD. Active listening is a valuable skill that can help improve communication in ADHD relationships. This involves giving your full attention to your partner when they are speaking and making an effort to understand their perspective.

Using "I" statements can also be helpful in ADHD relationships. Instead of blaming or criticizing your partner, express your feelings and needs using "I" statements. For example, instead of saying, "You never listen to me," try saying, "I feel unheard when I'm speaking, and it's important to me that we have open communication."

Avoiding distractions is another important communication strategy. Individuals with ADHD may be easily distracted by external stimuli, such as phones or television. Creating a distraction-free environment during important conversations can help improve focus and engagement.

Building Trust and Intimacy with ADHD

Trust and intimacy can be challenging in relationships affected by ADHD. The symptoms of ADHD, such as forgetfulness or impulsivity, can erode trust over time. Building and maintaining trust requires honesty and transparency. It is essential for individuals with ADHD to communicate openly about their struggles and limitations, while also taking responsibility for their actions.

Setting boundaries is another crucial aspect of building trust and intimacy in ADHD relationships. Both partners should have a clear understanding of each other's needs and expectations. This includes setting boundaries around time management, responsibilities, and personal space. Respecting these boundaries can help create a sense of safety and security within the relationship.

Prioritizing quality time together is also important for building intimacy in ADHD relationships. Making time for shared activities, hobbies, or date nights can help strengthen the emotional connection between partners. It is essential to create an environment where both partners feel valued and appreciated.

Managing Emotions in ADHD Relationships

Emotional dysregulation is a common challenge for individuals with ADHD. They may experience intense emotions or have difficulty managing their feelings effectively. This can impact relationships as emotional outbursts or mood swings may occur more frequently.

Mindfulness techniques can be helpful in managing emotions in ADHD relationships. Practicing mindfulness involves being fully present in the moment and observing one's thoughts and emotions without judgment. This can help individuals with ADHD become more aware of their emotional states and develop strategies for regulating them.

Self-care is another important aspect of managing emotions in ADHD relationships. Taking care of one's physical and mental well-being can help reduce stress and improve emotional regulation. This can include activities such as exercise, meditation, getting enough sleep, and engaging in hobbies or interests.

Seeking support is also crucial for managing emotions in ADHD relationships. This can involve reaching out to friends, family members, or support groups who understand the challenges of ADHD. Professional help, such as therapy or counseling, can also provide valuable tools and strategies for managing emotions in relationships.

Coping with ADHD-Related Impulsivity in Relationships

Impulsivity is a common symptom of ADHD that can have a significant impact on relationships. Individuals with ADHD may struggle with impulsive behaviors such as interrupting others, making impulsive decisions, or engaging in risky behaviors. These behaviors can strain relationships and lead to conflict or misunderstandings.

Coping strategies for impulsivity in ADHD relationships include practicing self-control. This involves taking a moment to pause and reflect before acting on an impulse. Setting goals and creating a plan can also help individuals with ADHD manage their impulsivity. Breaking tasks or decisions into smaller steps can make them more manageable and reduce impulsive behavior.

Seeking professional help is another important step in coping with impulsivity in ADHD relationships. Therapists or coaches who specialize in ADHD can provide guidance and support in developing strategies for impulse control. They can also help individuals explore the underlying causes of impulsivity and develop coping mechanisms.

Balancing Responsibilities in ADHD Relationships

Balancing responsibilities can be challenging in relationships affected by ADHD. The symptoms of ADHD, such as forgetfulness or difficulty with organization, can make it difficult for individuals to fulfill their obligations or contribute equally to household tasks.

Creating a schedule or routine can be helpful in balancing responsibilities in ADHD relationships. This can provide structure and help individuals with ADHD stay organized and on track. Delegating tasks and responsibilities can also help distribute the workload more evenly and reduce feelings of overwhelm or resentment.

Open communication is essential for balancing responsibilities in ADHD relationships. Both partners should have a clear understanding of each other's expectations and needs. Regular check-ins and discussions about household tasks or responsibilities can help ensure that both partners feel heard and supported.

Supporting Your Partner with ADHD

Support and understanding are crucial in ADHD relationships. It is important for partners to educate themselves about ADHD and its impact on relationships. This can involve reading books or articles, attending support groups, or seeking professional guidance.

Being patient and compassionate is also essential when supporting a partner with ADHD. It is important to remember that ADHD is a neurodevelopmental disorder and not a choice or character flaw. Celebrating your partner's strengths and accomplishments can help build their self-esteem and create a positive environment within the relationship.

Celebrating the strengths of ADHD relationships is another important aspect of support. Individuals with ADHD often possess unique qualities such as creativity, spontaneity, and passion. Recognizing and appreciating these strengths can help foster a sense of pride and empowerment within the relationship.

Addressing ADHD-Related Challenges in Family Relationships

ADHD can have a significant impact on family relationships as well. The symptoms of ADHD, such as forgetfulness or impulsivity, can create challenges in parenting, sibling dynamics, or extended family interactions.

Setting clear expectations is crucial in addressing ADHD-related challenges in family relationships. Clearly communicating rules, boundaries, and consequences can help individuals with ADHD understand expectations and reduce conflict within the family.

Seeking family therapy can also be beneficial in addressing ADHD-related challenges in family relationships. Family therapy provides a safe space for open communication, conflict resolution, and developing strategies for managing ADHD within the family unit.

Practicing self-care is another important aspect of addressing ADHD-related challenges in family relationships. Taking care of one's physical and mental well-being can help reduce stress and improve the ability to cope with the challenges of ADHD. This can include activities such as exercise, seeking support from friends or support groups, and engaging in hobbies or interests.

Navigating ADHD in Friendships and Social Connections

ADHD can also impact friendships and social connections. Individuals with ADHD may struggle with social skills, impulsivity, or forgetfulness, which can make it challenging to maintain friendships or navigate social situations.

Honesty and upfront communication are crucial when navigating ADHD in friendships and social connections. Being open about one's ADHD diagnosis or symptoms can help friends understand and accommodate their needs. Setting boundaries around social activities or commitments can also help individuals with ADHD manage their energy levels and avoid overwhelm.

Seeking support is important when navigating ADHD in friendships and social situations. Friends who understand the challenges of ADHD can provide valuable support and empathy. Support groups or online communities can also offer a sense of belonging and understanding.

Seeking Professional Help for ADHD-Related Relationship Issues

There may be times when seeking professional help is necessary to address ADHD-related relationship issues. If the challenges of ADHD are significantly impacting the quality of the relationship or causing distress for one or both partners, it may be beneficial to seek guidance from a therapist, coach, or support group.

Therapists who specialize in ADHD can provide valuable tools and strategies for managing the impact of ADHD on relationships. They can help couples develop effective communication skills, navigate conflict, and address underlying issues that may be contributing to relationship difficulties.

Coaches who specialize in ADHD can provide guidance and support in developing strategies for managing symptoms and improving relationship dynamics. They can help individuals with ADHD set goals, create routines, and develop coping mechanisms for challenges that arise within relationships.

Support groups for individuals with ADHD or their partners can offer a sense of community and understanding. These groups provide a space for sharing experiences, seeking advice, and receiving support from others who are facing similar challenges.

Celebrating the Strengths and Positives of ADHD Relationships

While ADHD can present challenges in relationships, it is important to recognize and celebrate the strengths and positives that come with ADHD. Individuals with ADHD often possess unique qualities such as creativity, spontaneity, and passion. These qualities can bring excitement and joy to relationships.

Encouraging a positive and empowering perspective on ADHD in relationships can help shift the focus from the challenges to the strengths. By recognizing and appreciating the positive aspects of ADHD, individuals can develop a sense of pride and self-acceptance.

Understanding and addressing ADHD in relationships is crucial for maintaining healthy and fulfilling connections. By implementing strategies for clear communication, building trust and intimacy, managing emotions, coping with impulsivity, balancing responsibilities, and providing support, individuals can navigate the challenges of ADHD in relationships. Seeking professional help when needed and celebrating the strengths of ADHD relationships can further enhance the quality of these connections. With understanding, patience, and compassion, individuals with ADHD and their partners can build strong and resilient relationships that thrive despite the challenges.

Chapter 23: From Chaos to Control

Executive functioning refers to a set of cognitive processes that are responsible for goal-directed behavior, problem-solving, and decision-making. It plays a crucial role in our ability to plan, organize, manage time, pay attention, and regulate our emotions. Strong executive functioning skills are essential for success in both academic and professional settings. In this article, we will explore the different components of executive functioning, the importance of developing these skills, and strategies for improving executive functioning.

Understanding Executive Functioning

Executive functioning can be defined as the set of mental processes that enable individuals to plan, organize, and execute tasks. It involves several interconnected components, including working memory, cognitive flexibility, inhibitory control, self-awareness, time management, decision-making, and emotional regulation.

Working memory is the ability to hold and manipulate information in our minds over short periods of time. It allows us to remember and use relevant information while performing tasks. Cognitive flexibility refers to our ability to adapt to changing situations and switch between different tasks or perspectives. Inhibitory control is the ability to suppress irrelevant or impulsive thoughts and behaviors.

Self-awareness is the ability to recognize and understand our own thoughts, emotions, strengths, and weaknesses. Time management involves the ability to prioritize tasks, allocate time effectively, and meet deadlines. Decision-making refers to the process of evaluating options and choosing the best course of action. Emotional regulation involves managing and controlling our emotions in order to respond appropriately to different situations.

The Importance of Executive Functioning for Success

Strong executive functioning skills are crucial for academic and professional success. Individuals with strong executive functioning skills are better able to plan and organize their work, manage their time effectively, stay focused and attentive, make informed decisions, regulate their emotions, and adapt to changing circumstances.

For example, students with strong executive functioning skills are more likely to excel academically because they can effectively manage their time, prioritize tasks, and stay focused on their studies. Similarly, professionals with strong executive functioning skills are more likely to be productive, meet deadlines, and make sound decisions in the workplace.

Many successful individuals attribute their achievements to their strong executive functioning skills. For instance, Elon Musk, the CEO of Tesla and SpaceX, has often credited his ability to think critically, solve complex problems, and manage his time effectively as key factors in his success. Similarly, Oprah Winfrey has spoken about the importance of self-awareness and emotional regulation in her journey to becoming a media mogul.

Identifying Weaknesses in Executive Functioning

Weak executive functioning skills can manifest in various ways. Some common signs of weak executive functioning include difficulty with planning and organizing tasks, poor time management, forgetfulness, impulsivity, difficulty staying focused or completing tasks, difficulty making decisions, and difficulty regulating emotions.

Individuals with weak executive functioning skills may struggle academically or professionally due to their difficulties with organization, time management, and task completion. They may also experience challenges in their personal lives, such as difficulty maintaining relationships or managing their emotions effectively.

Strategies for Developing Self-Awareness

Self-awareness is a fundamental component of executive functioning. It allows us to recognize our strengths and weaknesses, understand our emotions and motivations, and make informed decisions. Developing self-awareness can greatly improve our executive functioning skills.

One technique for developing self-awareness is journaling. Taking the time to reflect on our thoughts, emotions, and experiences can help us gain insight into ourselves and our patterns of behavior. Another technique is mindfulness meditation, which involves paying attention to the present moment without judgment. This practice can help us become more aware of our thoughts and emotions.

Seeking feedback from others can also be helpful in developing self-awareness. Asking trusted friends or colleagues for their observations and insights can provide valuable information about our strengths and weaknesses.

Building a Strong Foundation with Time Management

Time management is a critical aspect of executive functioning. Effective time management allows us to prioritize tasks, allocate time appropriately, and meet deadlines. Developing strong time management skills can greatly enhance our executive functioning abilities.

One tip for effective time management is to create a schedule or to-do list. Breaking tasks down into smaller, manageable chunks and assigning specific time slots for each task can help us stay organized and focused. It is also important to set realistic goals and deadlines, taking into account our own capabilities and limitations.

Another strategy for effective time management is to minimize distractions. This can involve turning off notifications on our phones or computers, finding a quiet and dedicated workspace, and using tools such as timers or productivity apps to stay on track.

Enhancing Focus and Concentration

Focus and concentration are essential for completing tasks efficiently and effectively. Improving our ability to focus and concentrate can significantly enhance our executive functioning skills.

One technique for improving focus and concentration is the Pomodoro Technique. This involves working in short bursts of focused activity, typically 25 minutes, followed by a short break. This cycle is repeated several times throughout the day. This technique helps to maintain focus by breaking tasks into manageable chunks and providing regular breaks for rest and rejuvenation.

Practicing mindfulness meditation can also improve focus and concentration. Mindfulness involves paying attention to the present moment without judgment. Regular practice can help train our minds to stay focused on the task at hand and reduce distractions.

Developing Effective Decision-Making Skills

Decision-making is a crucial aspect of executive functioning. Developing effective decision-making skills can greatly enhance our ability to plan, problem-solve, and achieve our goals.

One strategy for making effective decisions is to gather information and consider multiple perspectives before making a choice. This involves conducting research, seeking advice from trusted sources, and considering the potential consequences of different options.

Another technique is to use a decision-making framework, such as the pros and cons list or the decision matrix. These tools can help us evaluate the advantages and disadvantages of different options and make more informed decisions.

Managing Emotions and Stress

Emotions and stress can have a significant impact on our executive functioning abilities. Learning to manage our emotions and stress effectively can greatly improve our ability to think clearly, make decisions, and regulate our behavior.

One technique for managing emotions and stress is deep breathing. Taking slow, deep breaths can activate the body's relaxation response and help us calm down in stressful situations. Engaging in regular physical exercise, practicing relaxation techniques such as yoga or meditation, and seeking support from friends or professionals can also be helpful in managing emotions and stress.

Strengthening Working Memory

Working memory is a critical component of executive functioning. It allows us to hold and manipulate information in our minds while performing tasks. Strengthening our working memory can greatly enhance our ability to plan, problem-solve, and make decisions.

One exercise for improving working memory is the "dual n-back" task. This involves remembering a sequence of visual or auditory stimuli while simultaneously keeping track of the position of a target stimulus. Regular practice of this task can improve working memory capacity over time.

Another technique for improving working memory is to engage in activities that require mental effort and concentration, such as puzzles, reading, or learning a new skill. These activities challenge our working memory and help to strengthen it.

Improving Organization and Planning Abilities

Organization and planning are essential for effective executive functioning. Developing strong organization and planning skills can greatly enhance our ability to manage tasks, meet deadlines, and achieve our goals.

One strategy for improving organization is to create a system for keeping track of tasks and deadlines. This can involve using a planner or digital calendar, setting reminders or alarms, and breaking tasks down into smaller, manageable steps.

Another technique is to declutter and organize our physical and digital spaces. Having a clean and organized environment can help reduce distractions and improve focus.

Maintaining Consistency and Accountability

Consistency and accountability are crucial for effective executive functioning. Developing strategies to maintain consistency and hold ourselves accountable can greatly enhance our ability to stay on track and achieve our goals.

One technique for maintaining consistency is to establish routines and habits. This involves setting specific times for certain activities, such as waking up and going to bed at the same time each day, or scheduling regular exercise or study sessions.

Another strategy is to find an accountability partner or join a support group. Sharing our goals and progress with others can help us stay motivated and committed to our tasks.

In conclusion, executive functioning plays a crucial role in our ability to plan, organize, manage time, pay attention, and regulate our emotions. Strong executive functioning skills are essential for success in both academic and professional settings. By developing self-awareness, improving time management, enhancing focus and concentration, developing effective decision-making skills, managing emotions and stress, strengthening working memory, improving organization and planning abilities, and maintaining consistency and accountability, we

can greatly enhance our executive functioning skills and achieve our
goals.

Don't miss out!

Visit the website below and you can sign up to receive emails whenever Travis Breeding publishes a new book. There's no charge and no obligation.

https://books2read.com/r/B-A-CBXDB-CSEXC

BOOKS 2 READ

Connecting independent readers to independent writers.

Did you love *From Chaos To Control: How To Develop Strong Executive functioning Skills*? Then you should read *Celebrating Neurodiversity*[1] by Travis Breeding!

[2]

"Celebrating Neurodiversity" is not just a book; it's a manifesto for acceptance, understanding, and inclusivity. Breeding passionately advocates for the celebration of differences, urging readers to embrace the mosaic of neurodiversity that enriches our society. Through empowering stories of resilience, creativity, and innovation, Breeding showcases the immense potential that lies within the neurodivergent community.

From the unique ways in which neurodivergent individuals perceive the world to the invaluable insights they offer, "Celebrating Neurodiversity" is a thought-provoking exploration of what it truly

---

1. https://books2read.com/u/4DnjxP

2. https://books2read.com/u/4DnjxP

means to be neurodivergent. Breeding's empowering narrative inspires readers to challenge preconceived notions, foster empathy, and champion diversity in all its forms.

Whether you're a neurodivergent individual, a caregiver, or simply curious about the intricacies of the human mind, "Celebrating Neurodiversity" is a must-read that will leave a lasting impact. Join Travis Breeding on a journey of self-discovery, acceptance, and celebration as we embrace the kaleidoscope of neurodiversity and revel in the beauty of our differences.

Read more at breedingautismconsulting.com.

Also by Travis Breeding

Harmony in Flux: Navigating Bi-Polar Brilliance

The Friendship Rainbow

The Great Kindergarten Adventure: A Story about Going to School with Autism

The Magic Forest Adventure

Unlocking Brilliance: Navigating Autism and Applied Behavior Analysis Towards a Radiant Future

Decoding Love: Navigating Dating and Relationships on the Autism Spectrum

Echoes of a Late Diagnosis: Unveiling the Spectrum Within

From Theory to Practice: Implementing Effective Autism Interventions St

The Amazing Adventures of Aiden and His Asperger's Superpowers

The Magical Adventures of Lily and the Enchanted Forest

Unlocking Potential: A Journey Of Discovery Through ABA Therapy

Unlocking Potential: Navigating Employment for Neurodiverse Talent

Unlocking the Spectrum: A Journey through Applied Behavior Analysis from an Autistic Perspective

Unlocking The Spectrum: Navigating The Complexity Of Autism With Advanced Strategies And Insights

Beyond The Spectrum: Insights From Autistic Adults

Beyond The Stereotypes

Breaking Barriers: Navigating Autism With Therapeutic Insight

Celebrating Neurodiversity

Watch for more at breedingautismconsulting.com.

About the Author

Travis is the author of over 50 books about autism spectrum disorder. He travelst he country sharing the mission of making the world a better place for autistic individuals. In his spare time Travis enjoys writing, walking, and watching sports.

Read more at breedingautismconsulting.com.

www.ingramcontent.com/pod-product-compliance
Lightning Source LLC
Chambersburg PA
CBHW021435150726
47989CB00001B/254